INTENTIONAL

The Enemy's Stronghold on Minority Youth

J.Ridley

emerge
publishing

www.Emerge.pub

25 24 23 22 21 20   1 2 3 4 5 6 7 8

INTENTIONAL: THE ENEMY'S STRONGHOLD ON MINORITY YOUTH

Unless otherwise noted, all Scripture taken from the *King James Version* of the Bible.

Scripture quotations marked NIV are taken from THE HOLY BIBLE, NEW INTERNATIONAL VERSION®, NIV® Copyright © 1973, 1978, 1984, 2011 by Biblica, Inc.® Used by permission. All rights reserved worldwide.

Published by:

Emerge Publishing, LLC

9521B Riverside Parkway, Suite 243 Tulsa, Oklahoma 74137

Phone: 888.407.4447   www.EmergePublishing.com

Library of Congress Cataloging-in-Publication Data:

ISBN: 978-1-949758-76-4 Perfect Bound

"Our fear is not that we are inadequate,
Our fear is that we are powerful beyond
measure."

Marianne Williamson

The separation of church and state was made so we could
worship as each individual saw fit. So no one would be forced
into a one-size-fits-all box, like so many other countries.
The interpretation of this statement has made us rely
on the fact that God does not belong any other place
except in us, as a church. But God must be everywhere.
Jesus did not worship or teach in a building, but along His
journey out in the open.
We, individually, are His church.

TABLE OF CONTENTS

DEDICATION

First and foremost, I would like to thank my Heavenly Father
not only for giving me the courage and strength to share in
what He has done in my life, but also the boldness to speak
on the tactics of the enemy. I would like to thank my mother,
who has been a support to me and example of a strong
woman. My father for his encouragement. I could not have
done this without the love and wisdom of my son, who
always motivates me to be better in so many ways. My
mentee and princess Nancy a young lady whose heart is full
of compassion and is the epitome of resiliency. I also would
like to thank my pastor, Pastor Tim, and my church family.
They have been a foundation in my spiritual journey and
walk;
I would not be where I am if it weren't for their continuous
and unconditional love. There are two other pastors and faith
leaders I would like to thank, Pastor Joseph and Pastor Titus,
for always praying with me through the doubt and fear.
Last but not least, I would like to thank each and every young
person who has taught me to look beyond the surface, beyond
the walls, and into the hearts and souls within each of them.
This book is for you.

ACKNOWLEDGEMENTS

Nothing is ever created in isolation, and I would be remiss if I did not thank those who played a hand in the development of this book. First, I would like to thank my friend and sister in Christ Massiel Guttierez. Without her patience, love, and support, this book would not have been completed. To my mentor and also sister in Christ, Professor LeShelle Woodard. Your patience, guidance and love for the past sixteen years have given me strength to continue in exploring all of the talents God has given me. I would also like to thank Ken Evans whose love and support was significant in the completion of this book. I would like to thank Malik, whose poems are shared throughout the book. His plight and path are told in his ability to articulate the pain and realness of the enemy and the burden of young black men in this country. Last, I want to acknowledge a few of the young men I lost, M.R., A.D. and X.R-you have all taught me more than you know.

FOREWORD

We learn about God and His Redemptive Love through the Scriptures, and many of those Scriptures are simply stories. Indeed, these stories are what most of us remember, teach, and preach about as we attempt to draw people to Jesus. We have a certain advantage, however; this overarching theme of these stories is God's great love for His creation.

Ahead of you --if you're willing to take the journey-- is an intensely personal story of one of God's children, Janelle Ridley. Parts of her story will remind you of places in your life. Other parts will open your eyes to the world that far too many of our young people inhabit. This is the world, and these are the people where Janelle has been called to serve.

As our cities reel from protests and as our churches finally awaken to the truth of injustice that has plagued a significant portion of the American population for centuries, this book is a timely, truthful guide through the thoughts and behaviors of often, well-meaning people that produces the injustice and inequities that form this inequitable landscape; the place where these youths live.

If you don't like truth and transparency, or if seeing the Scriptures "lived out" in the lives of a real person is unappealing to you, put this book down and walk away. If, however, you want to see the "everyday" miracles of God in a young woman's life and in the lives of some of the most difficult to reach youth, turn the page.

You're in for the ride of your life.

Rev. David Wright
Executive Director of the Black Ministerial Alliance of Greater Boston
Assistant Pastor, Peoples Baptist Church of Boston
Adjunct Professor, Gordon Conwell Theological Seminary

PROLOGUE

Before I get into the depth of this book, I want to share with you the "why" for this book. I am nothing more than a Christian woman who has decided to share a bit of her world as she sees it. As a person who gave her life to Christ at the age of 16, but never fully entered into a relationship with God until 29, I don't pretend to know everything or have all the answers. This is just how my life's journey has led me to spreading the Word of Jesus Christ and the price He has paid, so we may know and experience our Heavenly Father's love. For the last few years, I have noticed things in my life that have made me stop and pay attention to His work. Unfortunately, it has made me see the "other" work as well. I have done a lot of reading and learning from inspirational leaders, such as Bishop T.D. Jakes, Dr. Tony Evans, Pastor Michael Todd, and others, such as local pastors who were placed to be shepherds for God's children. Their common purpose is to share the hope and love of God with those who need to know of Him. The reason for this book is the many young people my Heavenly Father has put before me. For their privacy, I will leave their names out, but without hesitation I will mention my son, LJ, who has been my strength in this process, and his adopted sister who I call "princess Nancy," and my mom, who has been an incredible support, which has given me the courage to finish this book.

God has shown me so much kindness, love, and grace, far beyond what I deserve, and I need to return the favor. I will begin by sharing a bit of my testimony because only then will you understand my "why" for this book.

As a young woman, I had always struggled with depression and anxiety. Low self-esteem led me to making choices I am not proud of, but I do not regret them either. As a person who did not know her worth in Christ, I have allowed people into my life who have done nothing but tear me down, weaken me, and use me for their own selfish gain. As painful as that is, I do not regret those paths or those people because they have taught me how to value those who do appreciate me and how to spot the wolf in sheep's clothing our Heavenly Father warns us of. I am not perfect, and because I suffered so much emotional dislike for myself and inner anger for not being strong enough, I have hurt people in my life who did not deserve it. As a woman of Christ, I now know the difference between doing things in my own strength and doing it in His. In Scripture, He tells us, "Come to me, all you who are weary and burdened, and I will give you rest" (Matthew 11:28 NIV). His way is so much better and easier. Although it is difficult to release control, it causes us less heartache in the end, and therefore we do not allow our emotions to dictate our choices and path. I have seen that He works out all things for the good, no matter how much of a mess we may have created. He also shows us that what the world and man mean for bad, He will always use for our good.

It has been the last four years of my life that I have begun my journey with Christ. But it has only been the last year that I have fully surrendered all areas of my life to Him. He has begun helping me to understand "me." I began to learn about myself when I was 32. That was when I was able to understand the circumstances in my life, the reasons behind the decisions I made, and how compassion and love need to be the driving force behind all I do. I have learned how to appreciate and value myself, which is not an easy journey for any individual because of the amount of work it takes, but also the pain you endure in dealing in truth.

I have learned that a lot of my past decisions were made in a place where I did not love myself or know my self-worth. As I started to realize this, I began taking a look at the people around me and realized that whether they admit it or not, they do not know their value or really love themselves either. I started taking a look at the path He has laid out, the young people He has placed in my life, and my heart began to break, but, at the same time, become full. He has entrusted me with young lives who are seeking hope, love, and purpose. I could not be more thankful for His love and confidence to build and instill within the lives of young people who have been torn down, beaten, and abused. As a former social worker, teacher, and administrator within the public school system, I realized young people have no idea how much value they hold. They do not understand that their present situation does not define the lives that they will live or prevent the blessing that God has waiting for them.

I remember reading Joyce Meyer's book *The Battlefield of the Mind* and learning about strongholds. The devil uses us for his pleasure, and our mind is his playground where he spends his time enjoying our pain. It was as if I could create the picture within my imagination of the devil on this swing set. He just sits there swinging, getting higher and higher, laughing and smiling. Every time he got me to believe something negative about myself was a pump of his legs on the swing; every time he got me to believe little of myself, he slid down the slide; and every time he was able to darken my days, he would gleefully laugh on the carousel as he went round and round. Every time he allowed me to become anxiety ridden when I had a public speaking engagement and I would tell myself how inadequate I was to be where I was, I empowered him. However, I have also learned he started his work with me when I was young, and it only grew as I got older. I gave him access to the most important thing, my mind, and I let him have fun. I have come to see that he is in the young people I work with. The barriers and challenges they face are the strongholds in their minds that he has created. Most of the time, I feel completely helpless that I can't rid them of these evil playgrounds. Young girls and boys are his targets, but for this book, I will focus on the boys.

Our young boys are his targets, and if we think about it, our boys have always been his targets. From the birth of Moses and the king's order for all male babies to be put to death to the birth of Christ and the order for all boys to be killed for fear of the Messiah existing, young males have had a mark on their heads. We have continued to allow history to repeat itself with the manifestation of those in charge fearing the loss of power in a new era. What I have witnessed the last few years is that the devil has waged war against our boys of color from the very young to the very old. He has set forth a war, and he is winning each battle. But I am here to tell you that Christ has died and won the war, but we need to do our part and fight back. We need to arm ourselves as He tells us in His Word. We need to know when we need to fight back and when He has called us to be still and let Him fight.

If we do not educate and armor ourselves with the Word and love of God, we are going to continue to lose each battle. We are going to lose our boys, and the world that was supposed to exist for them will, become the enemy's. I refuse to let him take my son or anyone else's. I hold true to His Word, that He sent His only begotten son, Jesus Christ, who tells us, "I have overcome the world" (John 16:33 NIV). We have won the war through Him, so why are we not holding on to this truth? Or are we choosing to forget this because we have lost sight of Him, His love, and the faith He tells us that we are to hold on to? This book is not the beginning of my purpose and pathway, but a start. It is one way for me to spread my hope and His message further.

I pray that this is well-received. I assure you it is well-intentioned. My love for young people is something I know has been embedded in my DNA makeup. My only goal is for all to know how loved and valued they truly are. To all my princes and princesses, as I like to call my children, it is time you start claiming the throne that has been awaiting you. It is our responsibility as the adults within their lives to get them there.

CHAPTER 1

The Accuser

I started my career as a social worker for the Department of Children and Families and worked for that agency a little more than six years. At that time in my life, I thought of myself as a Christian. I went to church, was engaged to be married to the first man I had truly dated, and was going to begin a life of being a good person God would be proud of. Well, ummm, that was not the case. I have always heard it said, if you want to make God laugh, tell Him your plans. That began my reality into the "darkness" our world holds. I was a 21-year-old recent college graduate who thought she knew everything. I was ready to wrap a red cape over my shoulders and save the world. I laugh as I write this because I still think I can save the world. I say that because God has given me a strength and a determination that does not allow me to think otherwise. Superwoman has nothing on me! I just refuse to give up, unless He directs me to do differently. That was the mindset I had then, and the one I continue to have.

I was in for a rude awakening. I had no idea what would await me when my life's work began in the fight for children. I tell everyone, when I worked for the department, I spent my first year crying and my second year angry. By the third year, my anger had turned to something else. I had turned into someone else. I became so desensitized by all that I had seen that my inner being was so numb and I lost a part of me. The darkness that I worked in had consumed me to the point I had questioned all that I knew and believed. My faith had diminished. I could not make sense of anything. It began to invade my personal life. I did not see the change within me coming. We usually don't. This is how the enemy works. It begins slow with frustration that turns into anger. Anger leads to bitterness and resentment.

I had given up hope and begun to blame and condemn the families I was serving for their own downfall and failure. I was fighting the parents for the corruption and trajectory of their children instead of taking the time to understand and see the systematic and structural racism that was at play. I had begun to see the world differently. The little relationship I did have with our Heavenly Father was gone. Like so many, I began to go through the routine of religion, rather than building the relationship He has asked us for. I began to question everything. How could a Heavenly Father who claims to love us allow children to be sexually abused? What did these children do to deserve a life filled with violence and abuse? How do people kill people they love? How do adults choose their own pleasure before their child? Why couldn't the parents understand that their lives are not their own? That they have to do what is best for their children?

Then I was reminded to go back to the beginning, to Genesis 1:27-28 "So God created mankind in His own image, / in the image of God, He created them; / male and female he created them. / God blessed them and said to them, 'Be fruitful and increase in number, fill the earth and subdue it'" (NIV). Subdue means to overcome or bring under control. In Genesis, He tells us that He gave us dominion over the earth. You see, God gave us as His children/humans the choice of how we live and how we treat what He has entrusted to us, which is this world. Unfortunately, when angels fell, so did we. He continued to allow us to choose how we love and live. He did not create any of the situations or circumstances that are evil; He does, however, allow them to happen. Why? That is not a question I fully know the answer to, but I would point you in the direction of His shepherds that might be better suited to answer that question. I do promise you this: you will one day get to ask Him. However, it is a tactic the enemy does use to take our eyes off of things and begin to "accuse" everyone and everything for the despair in our lives or the lives of others.

I began to question the adolescents who were on my caseload about the choices that they made, and tell myself, "They can choose to do differently if they want to; they are just using their life as an excuse." I started comparing them to me. I was raised by a young single mother, who had me at the age of 18, then my brother two years later. My mother, who was not born here, had to learn and adapt to a new country. She had no idea what awaited her as a young mother, but she sacrificed and did all she could to provide for my brother and me.

Again, I (age 23 at this point) had considered myself to be a pretty perfect person who had it all figured out. It sounds so ridiculous to me now, but I have to speak my truth in order for you to understand His work in my life and the opening of my eyes. The judgments I had passed on clients, and young people, were the same judgments I had passed on everyone around me. From family to friends to co-workers, I thought I had them, and life, all figured out. Isn't it wonderful how the enemy gets us to believe in the most obsolete, but yet, because we are human, we all fall every time. I learned in the original language of the Bible that "Satan" means "accuser"—a person who claims that someone has committed an offense or done something wrong. We don't realize when the shift happens that we make ourselves our own idols, and therefore we stop looking to the one true God. We begin to blame others for their downfall and own demise, saying that they chose their path.

This is what he has done to our children. The enemy has allowed our children to believe in their own judgment and righteousness rather than what is correct and pure. This generation is growing further and further from the church, and any relationship with Jesus that they have was not taught correctly with the understanding of the difference between religion and relationship. We are not the judges of this world, but rather, we will one day be judged by the only living God who has the right to praise or condemn us for our actions, behavior, and how we used our time. This generation has been born into a time where all information is within its grasp. The problem is they are self-teaching and following those who are not conveying the correct information. The church has a tremendous age gap, and this current generation is not being raised with the foundation of God and Christ.

Our kids are walking the earth and moving along in the physical, but a part of them died long ago. When the stare of a young person is so dark that it chills you to the core, how do you pretend not to notice? How do you breathe life back into someone whose soul has been devoured by our society? We as a country, as a society, have dug countless graves for these young bodies, particularly our young men who are falling every day. I believe in this statement: our young people are existing, but they are not living. They are walking around with no hope and see no way out. Darkness has consumed them, and the light at the end of the tunnel was an old dream they had that kept moving further and further away until it disappeared.

It has made it easy for the enemy to convince young people that life has done them wrong, that there are folks out there who committed offenses against them, so he isolates them, convincing them they only have themselves and are justified in their actions. The enemy tempts you into sin, and when you commit the sin, he convinces you that you are unworthy of forgiveness and redemption. When you have no understanding of who you are, it's easy for the enemy to use the world to tell you who you are. I know, because for the longest time, the world convinced me of who I was and who I was not. I thank God for His truth and reminding me who He is, and because I know who He is, I know who I am and who I am not. I no longer need to fall prey to those bent on creating their version of who they believe me to be or who I should be.

Since the beginning, we have seen the attack among our boys and their destruction. The devil, since the beginning of time, has been intentional about his war, who and where he is targeting. The target is our young men because of the power they hold. The plan does not have to be against women because he knows that if he takes our men, our sons, our fathers, our husbands, that we as women will suffer and die within our own being. In Genesis, the Bible tells us that God created us in His image. However, when God created man, He realized the significance of breathing a life within that man. So He created woman to do that by pulling her out of him. Women are the completion of men. Women are the breaths of life in men, the ones who nurture them, and who fill them. By taking a man from a woman, a woman whose being is of love, you have removed a part of her.

You see, the devil knows our weaknesses, our fears, and our wants and therefore knows where to attack. So, the pain of mothers who lose their children to systems, streets, and sin-lived graves, looms in their thoughts as to where things could have gone wrong. Women begin to internalize, self-destruct, and cause self-harm by harboring the guilt and pain they feel. As mothers, they feel judgment and failure for not having done better to protect their children, for not being around enough, when the reality is that they had to work multiple jobs to provide. They feel guilt for not protecting their children from societal structures because they could not afford to live in the areas that would not allow darkness to creep in and plant seeds that would lead to danger. The condemnation they felt led them to stray from the church. The guidance they were seeking from the church made them feel ashamed of what was going on in their homes, which also made them lose faith in the church. When you are not planted in His Word, and know God's truth, you tend to believe those who are meant to help and lead His people. As my pastor tells me, they are men, they are human. They fall subject to the same sins and temptations we do. He also warns us that Jesus doesn't know everyone who says, "Lord, Lord, did I not prophesy in your name, did I not drive out demons and heal the sick?" (see Matthew 7). He tells us that not everyone is of Him even if they claim to be.

As I look at the number of young men of color within our justice system and the complacency that has engulfed them into the belief that this is normal, it reminds me of the book of Genesis through the book of Numbers. The story of Moses and the Israelites begins in the book of Genesis. Moses was the prophet chosen to deliver the Israelites from Pharaoh's command. Moses led them out of Egypt from captivity, bondage, and slavery to the promised land where they were to endure a life of freedom, blessings, peace, and joy. Moses, despite his doubt and insecurities and disbelief within himself, went to Pharaoh and demanded the release of his people. He warned Pharaoh of what was to come. They were profit for Pharaoh, and he stood to lose what he had if he let them go. He stood his ground and did not release the Israelites until he and his wife lost their son to God's final warning. Pharaoh's wife had begged and pleaded for Pharaoh to change his mind and release the Israelites before the death of her son, but Pharaoh, like so many, believed he was untouchable. We think because we hold a title, power, prestige, or money that we are exempt from things happening within our lives. God is clear: we are not exempt from anything.

Those who profit off of our justice system today are no different than Pharaoh. If we look at this definition clearly -- "accuser: a person who claims that someone has committed an offense or done something wrong" -- isn't that us? Every day in this country, people make accusations with no evidence, which has placed our young people in the emotionless, empty, entitled being that poses a real threat to future generations and our world as a whole.

Although it has been stated that there is no accuracy to the fact that prisons are built based off third grade standardized testing, there is research that shows the trajectory for young people who are not reading on grade level by the third grade leads to gaps in education and system involvement. Our young people are dying physically, emotionally, intellectually and, most important, spiritually. As adults, we are guilty of allowing this. So, why are we not being punished? Why do the adults get to lie in bed and sleep peacefully, while our babies are hurting and crying each day to the point that they have chosen a trajectory that leads to death? Whether that statement is literal in the notion that our children play god and determine their final day or they have passed judgment on those around them and are being killed because of it. These boys are living lives much bigger than them, and it is shortening their life span. They have shut out all hope, and any ounce of love they knew, to become a dead entity that is just borrowing space within a body -- a body of color that has a constant struggle to survive.

It is easy to lay fault with our young people that they made their beds and now they must lie in them. But the reality is we have given them the beds to make. When nothing else has been afforded to them, and they have not been shown differently, the only thing they can do is lie in them. We are in a country that does not believe in being accountable for its actions. To maintain some form of integrity, passing blame and flame "accusing" is easier to do than realize we have lost our humanity and compassion.

Paulo Freire in his book *Pedagogy of the Oppressed* states: Dehumanization, which marks not only those whose humanity has been stolen, but also those who have stolen it, is a distortion of the vocation of becoming more fully human … Because it is a distortion of being more fully human, sooner or later being less human leads to the oppressed to struggle against those who made them so. In order for this struggle to have meaning, the oppressed must not, in seeking to regain their humanity, become oppressors of the oppressors, but rather restorers of the humanity of both. (Freire, Paulo; Pedagogy of the oppressed, 2000)

When the purpose of our survival depends on the weak to remain so, we have demonstrated that we will choose self. We teach our kids not to bully, we teach our kids to tell us the truth, we teach our kids to think for themselves, but we do not teach our kids that we have to remain accountable at all times no matter how difficult the circumstance. We are holding our young people to a standard that we do not hold ourselves to. One day, we will be held in judgment. No matter what you believe, judgment comes, and it comes from the only one who matters -- our Heavenly Father. Right now, we are manipulating judgment here on earth; maybe it is through our boss on the integrity of our work.

To the parents who are raising children on the decisions and choices they make in life and manipulate the Bible to keep their children "in line" or "on the right track" and to "scare them into doing as told," it's meant to keep the children in order. What they do not realize is that it is actually drawing their child further from God than to Him. I have had several students and mentees of mine tell me over the years that they went to church because their parents forced them to. They resented their parents for it and therefore never understood why it was important to build a relationship. However, the church is full of people who, like me, did not know the difference between religion and a relationship. We begin to lose them at home before we lose them elsewhere.

Our world continues to oppress and conform. In school, teachers and leaders tend to conform or oppress for actions that do or do not align with the school's views, policies, or rules. It is not an accident that most students in special education are children of color. When adults do not understand that emotional, mental, and spiritual chaos could mirror "societal discourse" or who don't know how to communicate with students who have a different understanding of life, it is easier to see them as an abnormality rather than admit you may not be best suited to educate and determine the trajectory for that young person's life.

I understand a hierarchy must exist in order for function, in order for structure, to maintain the sanctity of order. However, when we are in a time where we have the most advanced technology and are creating the unthinkable, how is it that we have not managed to put an end to injustice? Our boys are wandering through a period where they are not deciding for themselves how their future is shaped. Because we have not learned from our past, things continue to repeat themselves. Slavery may have been abolished in the United States in 1863, but we are in a new era of bondage, similar to the wilderness period the Israelites walked through. The reason for their journey was that they were not making the necessary changes within themselves, and especially within their mentality. The only reason they did not reach the promised land sooner was not because they were lost within the physical, but because they were lost mentally and forgot who they were and what was promised for them. They forgot they were the princes, princesses, kings, and queens of the one Most High.

The mind is the devil's playground, where we are taught and learn to do our own self-damage. We don't need much assistance from others to push those thoughts along because we have done a pretty good job of deciding who we are based on what we have been dealt and what we have heard, how society treats us as individuals and the standards they have given us. Until we decide the truth of who we are, it leaves too much room for others to depict and change that picture. When we begin to hope within us and show our young people how to emulate that, we will begin to see a shift in our country. No one person is an accident. Each person has a divine destiny waiting to be filled, and none of that is meant for evil, heartache, and pain. We will have trials and challenges, but how we choose to handle and respond to them is a testimony to our character.

I have at times struggled with the trials and challenges set before me. Young women of color face inevitable trials and challenges. There are those who question your competency to do good work with a proven risk population if you are not of a certain social class and have lived experience, if you do not have the correct credentials, if you are perceived as being too young and naïve because you believe in being innovative, if you are attractive. But most importantly, the trials and challenges will come when you surpass all of that and stand strong in your conviction.

We need to own our story and forget the mentality society has placed on us. When we as people of color begin to take ourselves seriously, when we stop seeing ourselves as slaves and begin to liberate and free our minds, we can unite and have the rest of the world see us as God's children. Our young people are not together, our people of color are not together; we will continue to go through the wilderness until we break the strongholds within us. We will not leave the wilderness era and enter the promised land until we understand that it is what you leave in our young people, and not what you leave for them, that matters. In this country, less than 1 percent of people of color have generational wealth, but we are comprised of the generational achievement gap. How is it that we are on two ends of the spectrum, yet we expect young people to continue to fight and be the change makers?

CHAPTER 2

The Terrorist Inside

When I describe the work I do, I intentionally use the word "normal" because the definition of normal is "conforming to a standard; usual, typical or expected." The definition is so broad and vague that it is open to interpretation. However, the one word that strikes me is conform; that is the expectation I believe most adults have of young people -- that they will just fall in line. It is currently what is straining the relationships among our young boys of color and education. Both groups, young people and educators, have different ideas of what that word means and how it is used. The term, "normal," is broken down by class, race, culture, and gender. If teachers are not familiar with the community and culture of the young people they are educating, guiding, mentoring, and assisting, normalcy will strain the relationship because they and their students believe their definition of normal is the right one. In reality, neither have been exposed to each other's "normal" to understand the other's reality. In hindsight, both individuals are correct in what they consider normal behavior, standards, expectations, community, environment, and so forth. The challenge is both sides need to understand what each other's definition of "normal" is in order for the relationship to remain intact, helpful, and fruitful.

We are living in a time when slavery in any form should not exist. In a world that is rapidly changing, growing, and cultivating new minds, we still perpetuate the hidden, but very conscious, idea that individuals of color need to remain within the "hierarchy" that Anglo-Saxon systems have created. The systematic challenges and barriers will remain because they are intentionally put in place to keep a status quo that will produce a fruitful outcome for those in positions of power. The idea that our young men of color are not of the higher standard, class, and intellect, and the need for them to view their struggles the same as their white counterparts because the access, challenges, and opportunities are vastly different.

The world is feeding off of black and brown boys and men at war with each other. Where do we see any unity among those of color? The devil has continued to allow his soldiers to grow through racism and prejudice, leaving an unequal battle. Let me be clear that I am not saying whites are the devil's soldiers. Any individual who places him- or herself above another does not walk in the spirit of love. Whether you are of spiritual belief or not, that statement applies to each individual. In this world, we have titles, positions, and wealth that dictate our sense of importance. The problem with that is the world may think of you in that manner, but when you start behaving as if your life is of more value than another, that is where the trouble begins and that initial statement holds true. It may be an uncomfortable truth to swallow, but we do not live in a comfortable world.

Shackles, lynchings, whippings, and kidnappings do not need to occur anymore, but, because the devil has continued to manage a way of holding people captive mentally, he gains power, and enslavement continues to exist. The mind is the most powerful weapon that exists: no artillery, machine, or invention can break, destroy, or damage like the power of a strong mind or, in these young men's cases, a fragile and impressionable mind. This is what most of society knows and refuses to teach.

Paul, one of God's greatest disciples, was a man who killed, whipped, kidnapped, and employed every tactic of the enemy, yet managed to learn how to break that stronghold. After his encounter with God on the road to Damascus, his eyes being opened by the Lord, Paul writes of the strongholds, the devil's tactics, ones he fell prey to for several years. His only request and message throughout his writings is knowing what that looks like and how to combat it. Even in prison, Paul did not let the enemy hold him captive. Prison doors were shaken open, walls were broken, but yet, Paul did not leave prison. Instead, he began to sing. He sang and worshipped the Lord because, you see, he was never actually in prison. Physically, yes, but that was all. Mentally, spiritually, and emotionally, he was free. It did not matter his location because he had what he needed: his mind.

With a strong mind rooted and grounded in who you are, nothing can destroy you. We live in a country that makes billions of dollars off of the weaknesses of the mind. From the medical world, with those who are dealing with depression or suffering from some form of mental health condition, to the beauty industry, which is convincing people of what they should look like, how skinny they should be, what their body shape should look like, to the fashion industry and what you must have in order to be considered significant, noticed, or fitting in. The world is full of messages telling you who you should be and what you should have to the point it is destroying our kids. They are running down a path that is crippling them mentally just so they will be valued enough by others in order to hear that they matter.

Where we as humans fall short is in our decisions, judgments, and prejudices based on our circumstances. The question could be asked: What would you do for your rent/mortgage payment? What would you do to provide food for your children or even yourself? It's easy to find solutions when it's not a reality for you, but a person in desperation is not always able to reason and rationalize. For younger people, the ability to think logically in a still-forming brain is not and cannot be the expectation. Rather, it is necessary to give them the tools and skills they need to understand the choices and consequences of the hard decisions they need to make.

We live in a world of unspoken normalcy. Where it is normal for young boys of color to shoot at one another, to fight with one another and kill one another, for no reason other than what they perceive as necessary for survival? Whether you agree or not, young people who kill with no fear or regard for their lives are not normal. Whether they are killing because it's generational and they are the unfortunate inheritors of family dysfunction and discord, or whether it is because of structural barriers that have been set up to ensnare them in traps to continue to profit off of the backs of people of color, the rage is engrained within them. Because as the generations continue to grow, they grow further and further from the churches which means they have not heard of Jesus Christ or the Good News.

But they do not know any better. No individual wakes up every day wanting a life filled with fear. No child grows up wanting to be a criminal. If they do, what was the message they received? Young people, and most of the world, do not know the battle that has been waged on them. This battle is much larger than most realize. We are continuing a cycle of hate that is a normalcy and reality for them and this country. Brotherly love, kindness, respect, and true bonding are things that they do not know of because those things have not been demonstrated for them. From the communities that they live in, to the television shows they watch, to the news and media they hear—all they know is self-gratification and entitlement, and worse, judgement. We have shown young people that our thoughts, biases, and perceptions are what matters and that those concepts dictate outcomes. Our Heavenly Father tells us in Luke 9:25 "What good is it for someone to gain the whole world, and yet lose or forfeit their very soul." The price of peace is something the world cannot buy, power cannot obtain, and prestige cannot inherit. It is only through the mercy and grace of our Heavenly Father. It's one He will not give until we learn to humble ourselves and live as His children. We pretend to know everything when in truth, we are always learning because the world, things, and people are constantly changing. The answers of 20 years ago are not as relevant today as they were then. Yet, we have fears of admitting we don't know something, that we don't always have an answer, in shame of being judged or looked on as less than. For some, it's about being irrelevant and not needed.

Living for each day, repeating cycles and expecting things to be the same is the reality of our young people. They have it in their minds that they will not get caught. For most others, living for each day, doing the same thing, and expecting different outcomes is the hope. Although we live for each day, we need to hope for tomorrow because it is not promised to us. We must do differently to change the outcome. Young people do not hope for anything. They do not know how to plan for their future because they do not expect to make it that long. And if they do, they do not know what life could look like outside of what they know now. I have heard the statement, "The eyes are the window to the soul." The darkness or the light within one's eyes can reveal a person's character. But the eyes are also windows and doors. They can allow good things in, but they can also allow bad things. It is important to guard ourselves from those spirits vying to inhabit our soul. When I look into my young people's eyes and see the emptiness, it disturbs me. I see nothing but rage, anger, and bitterness, which leaves me wondering, "Where did we go wrong?"

I say "we" because it is not just one adult who fails a young person. We are currently in an epidemic that many discuss, though few acknowledge its severity. Fatherless children are currently an ongoing crisis and what most would consider an epidemic in America. The definition of epidemic is "the widespread occurrence of an infectious disease in a community at a particular time." Among the black and brown community, especially those in urban dwellings, the vast majority of homes consist of single mothers or other female relatives raising young boys. In 2017, according to US Census Bureau, there are more than 24 million children being raised in a single-parent home in the United States. One in four children are growing up without a father.

A normal part of childhood is figuring out your identity, and most do so by looking to their parents. They look at their physical features and point out similarities. They look at their interests and share those commonalities of their parents. They look at certain characteristics/personality traits and learn what is embedded within their makeup. I think about my son and his development over the years, his noticing of what features were similar to his dad's and mine. Or his love of sports and interest in activities that he could share in with each of us, not because we enjoyed it, but because he knew where his love of it came from. I watched as he tried to mimic certain behaviors of his dad, like not untying his shoes and wiggling his feet to slide them in, and using his index finger to pop his foot all the way in. The point is kids try to mirror the adults in their life, intentionally and unintentionally; it's a healthy and normal part of every human development.

Not knowing some part of your biological makeup, from a physical stance to an inner personality reflection, leaves one to create those thoughts on their own. It also leaves whoever is raising young people to impart their belief on where certain characteristics have come from. Too many kids hear, "You are just like your father: a no good deadbeat," or "You are going to end up just like your father, with no life, no goals, and in jail." Single parents do not leave strong images for their children because of the bitterness, anger, and resentment they have. Young people will assume the worst, then self-reflect on whether they exude those same characteristics that do not leave a strong example to build upon themselves.

Unfortunately, school, a place where you are supposed to learn your passions, strengths, and weaknesses—all which contribute to one's identity—does not always provide that. In addition to knowledge, education should give a sense of understanding of who you are as an individual through the development of your skills, talents, and creativity. But the battle begins early through the misconceptions, diagnoses, labels, and biases that are placed on students, especially young men of color. A battle starts early in our young people and education that is not rooted in positive identity development falls victim to the enemy. This lands young people in the enemy's territory early, when they are not even aware of it. If they are not aware, how can they prepare and fight?

I have heard many colleagues and adults who plead, pray, post, and tweet about their belief in and love for God. It is not for me to judge or assume how deep or how strong their relationship with God is. I struggle when I see them claim to be children of God and quote His Scriptures, yet they do not know or understand what it is to think of yourself less, that humility is putting others before you. It makes me question whether Christ is in them, or is it more about them wanting to convey a perception to the world and others?

However, if we believe in God, should there even be the question that darkness exists? Darkness is as real and as present as God. I need to stress this point because it is the darkness that has grabbed hold of our young ones. To some, it is obvious which young people are street involved, or have fallen into a life that could have a negative impact their trajectory. The darkness also cannot be so clear and evident to a lot of them. There are some young people (and adults) who are able to portray an identity that, while misleading, is raging in the enemy. It has such a grip that those young people are known to some who have done the direct work on the ground, the "after dark kids." They are saying that during the day, our young ones can present in one manner, and some will not suspect that these same kids have a secret life at night when they become the people who hold a strong, looming presence in our streets and neighborhoods. That their essence and name brings about fear and terror to those around them. If that does not sound like the darkness our Heavenly Father warns us can quickly entangle anyone, then I don't know what you think evil looks like.

I think we get confused as to what light and darkness are. We allow movies and society to depict grandiose visions for us. If we think long and hard, and open our eyes to the times we are in, we can see the light and darkness in our lives. When we ignore the deaths and imprisonment of young people, the suicide rates among children, and the widening gaps of inequities, that is part of the darkness that harbors within a person because they are choosing not to address it when our very being was created to bring light into those whose lives need it. My intent here is not solely for the captured darkness of young ones, but also the captured darkness of adults who abuse power and consider themselves judges of right and wrong.

When we ignore situations and the darkness in front of us, the devil has won. We have become self-absorbed with things are not our problem. I admit that I was one of those people. If it did not pertain to my world and did not impact me directly, I did not want to be involved with it. I used to believe that people had control over their situations and did not fight hard enough to overcome their situations. As a social worker, when I would look over case history and see the generational cycle of darkness, it became clear that people will only do what they know. If people and families do not know differently, they cannot teach differently, so nothing different will happen. They also cannot love differently.

It isn't until we grab hold of one generation for dear life and do not let go, not let them fall back into the world of darkness, that we stand a chance of different to occur. My young boys are struggling with the concept of manhood. For many, providing for their family is a way of life for them, but the expectation of boys making adult decisions is what is causing us to lose them. When will we realize we need to stop putting the burden of responsibility on our children? When do we allow our children to grow and be their age and condemn this notion that they are men when they are not? I do not want them to be men before their time; they are not ready for it. That it is evident by the numbers of young boys we have locked up. Statistics show that a large population of men ages 27 to 24 are incarcerated. In 2017, 33 percent of the men incarcerated within Boston ranged in age from 18-24, with that percentage increasing. According to statistics and data collected by the National Association for the Advancement of Colored People (NAACP), there are three million people in jail and prison today, far outpacing population growth and crime. Between 1980 and 2015, the number of people incarcerated increased from roughly 500,000 to 2.2 million. Despite making up close to 5% of the global population, the U.S. has nearly 25% of the world's prison population. African Americans and Hispanics represent 32 percent of the US population, but 56 percent of the US prison population. Our country has outranked other countries with the most people in incarceration.

The daily battles are constant and fierce with not many willing to bring light to the war that is brewing. It's becoming a conflict we can't continue to fight on our own until our soldiers outnumber his. A new leader rises up each battle to continue to gain the souls of our children. Each leader that rises is stronger than the other, and at times, I am falling to the darkness, with thoughts of taking those individuals out. But I have to remember, it is the leader who needs to see an increase in those who are aligning with God's work and purpose. The story of David and Goliath echoes in my mind, of the young man with five stones, a young man no one saw coming. Not only was he discouraged by those around him from going into battle, but he was not even considered capable to be a soldier. But the calling of the Almighty Father drowns every human being's thoughts and decisions and reigns over all. He called David into battle, armed him with what he needed, and used the unexpected to bring down a giant everyone feared.

Some of our young people are David. Some have ideas on what a "David" should look like, so many go unnoticed, unseen for the potential they have. They are overlooked, rendered incompetent, and discouraged because their means of handling challenges are not what others would deem as battle worthy or able to win. The foresight they have is significant, but their ability to execute is what is lacking and causes them to stumble. They are hindered, not because they do not have the ability to be great, to lead, or to make change. There aren't enough Saul's to give them the opportunity to go forth, to believe in them, and present the access.

Our young people are a mirror of what they see. They mirror the actions and thoughts deflected onto them in school. They are an image of what is occurring in their home. They are a reflection of the stereotype and perpetuation of their community. Our young people of color exist because they are always seen, but they are not living because they are not heard. The one thing our boys and girls of color are not seen as is the reflection of love that they were created to be. Reproduction is supposed to be an intimate act of love between two people, no matter how young or dysfunctional they may be. It is still real and true that the physical act of reproduction occurs between those who share some form of feelings toward one another, no matter how distorted it may be. Our young people reap the aftermath of what was sown. How fair is that? Our babies did not ask to be here; they were created to be here. Whether or not you agree in the living Jesus Christ, the Virgin Mother Mary is not the reality for all of these brown and black girls and boys.

CHAPTER 3

The Invisible War

My path has led me to my current career, where I work with young men and women in the juvenile justice system. My heart aches for them because they are so lost and don't even know it. Each one of these young men are dealing with some form of mental health condition, whether it is due to their environment, community, schools, home, or through their own personal struggle. Our children do not know who they are or their value. The mind is the battlefield, and it's where the battles of the enemy are beginning. Each day, we are losing our children. They disregard life because they do not appreciate their own. That is a problem. That is a crisis. That is our fault.

Each adult plays a role in a young person's life and is responsible in some part for their destruction. My one request of adults who work with children is if you are incapable of building, do not tear down and make them worse. You see, from my children I have learned and seen the pain they are not willing to admit they have. They are so numb that they cannot feel. They self-medicate by smoking and drinking because it is the only way to get through each day. It is no different than adults who abuse alcohol and drugs.

My heart cannot carry all of them, and here is where every adult can take pieces. Affirming a young person is not hard. It gets difficult when we allow our judgment to seep in and decide they are not worthy of affirmation. The problem with that is most adults only see part of that young person. They forget that these young people are kids who never got to experience being a child.

Now, some may say that there are many stories of those who have overcome trials and tribulations and did not divert to a dark path. However, not each individual is the same, and what each one carries is determined by the strength of their battlefield (mind) and how many soldiers are on their side. I will share examples throughout this chapter of young men who have agreed to share their stories with me. I will not use their names, but a pseudo name for each one. This is Malik's poem where he discusses the war within his mind, and this is true for every person I know, young and old. It gives credence to my statement on where the devil's playground and battlefield is and where the true war begins.

Malik vs. Mooky

The streets call me Mooky, mom calls me Malik
Mooky is a statistic, Malik is unique
Mooky get it out the mud, rain, snow or sleet

Malik is the rose that arose from the concrete.
Mooky is a felon for firearms possession
Mooky is a prisoner to his own aggression
Mooky abused drugs 'cuz he suffered from depression
Mooky plays a part in black adolescent oppression.

Malik's calculating, he isn't thirsty for attention
Malik's tired of nightmares, he's yearning for redemption
Malik deals with constant visit from evil spirits not to mention
But Malik never lets the pressure push him from his vision.
Malik's pursuing love that all he wanna feel
Mooky's playing with emotions a heart he might steal
Malik's apologizing for his ego your wounds he will heal
But Mook's a wolf in sheep's skin who only wants to kill
Malik fights Mook and the winner takes the throne
Mooky's always afraid 'cuz deep down he feels alone
'Cuz Malik's losing family where his house was once a home
They just wanna break the cycles that they feel are set in stone.

I believe mental health is a stronghold. The weakness found within us to question our existence is where the devil gets his fuel. The more we feel inadequate, the less likely we are to persevere. If we do not persevere, we will never live our God-given purpose with the sense of peace and joy that was meant for us. That is exactly what the devil wants, and if you can't see the impact he is having in Malik's life … No matter how much anyone in Malik's life tries to rebuild him, they face an army that outnumbers them and began their stronghold long before we entered his life.

We were created for a purpose and meant to live in peace. A Scripture that I hold on to each day and through each battle is Jeremiah 29:11 (NIV), which clearly tells us, "'For I know the plans I have for you,' declares the Lord, 'plans to prosper you and not to harm you, plans to give you hope and a future.'" Why don't we hold true to this in our hearts and in our minds? Mental health is a crisis in our nation. In 2014, the statistics show that one in five adults had some form of mental illness. That is more than 40 million adults in this country. In 2011, the rate of youth depression was 8.5 percent, but it increased to 11.1 percent in 2014. One in four people worldwide will suffer from some form of mental illness, which makes mental illness the leading cause of poor health and disabilities. The devil's playground is not apparent in these young boys because society has labeled them as angry, violent, ignorant, manipulative, and combative. So there is no thought to what these young men have gone through and continue to experience mentally and emotionally. He wins his battles by playing his games in their heads, forcing them to believe the worst about themselves. (Socio-economic class contributes to how we view our lives and self-worth; however, if that was the only factor, why would millionaires and celebrities check into hospitals for treatment each year?)

In the years working with the child welfare system, my time as a high school teacher, and now working more directly with incarcerated youth, the things that I have seen have convinced me that our young people have allowed society to influence how they feel about themselves. Not only have their environments played a role, but we as adults have affirmed it. I had labeled my young people as having a diagnosis of "street trauma," which by Wikipedia and Urban Dictionary combining the two words gives the definition "the culture of inner city neighborhoods, which causes a deeply distressing or disturbing experience." We have contributed to the decline of their self-image and self-worth, therefore contributing to the decline in their mental health. When we deny EVERY young person the right to be who they are, we are contributing to that mental chaos within them. When we deny kids opportunities that should be afforded to everyone, we are contributing to their mental chaos. When we punish kids for not knowing the difference between right and wrong because their sense of normal is what is right, we are contributing to their mental chaos. When we lock up kids because in their world, black and brown people are supposed to behave in a certain manner to be noticed, respected, and of worth, we are contributing to their mental chaos.

During my time working as a substitute teacher in an inner-city high school, the amount of dysfunction I had seen led me to question how far we have strayed from God's Word or, better yet, human compassion. These young people portray an act of toughness and courage that really is a mask to protect themselves from the pain and hopelessness they feel. What I noticed throughout my career working with young people is the self-hatred they endure. Young people do not have the capacity to demonstrate love or to identify it because they have neither felt nor seen it. They have seen lust, which is why it is easy for them to engage in multiple relationships, or move quickly from one person to another. They have seen loneliness, which is why they need to be around others even when they know that person or environment is harmful, and they have seen manipulation by adults to dictate or control outcomes in their favor as a means of worth or survival. The generational cycle that has been ongoing in our country of single-parent households, poverty, homelessness, and being system-involved is at an all-time high. We are reproducing and producing generations of emotionless young people. A young lady who entered my path for a short time, who goes by the name Indigo, said to me:

"I have never been welcomed anywhere in my life. I am always the extra mouth they didn't want to feed; I was the kid who was always in trouble and eventually became that kid that didn't feel. If I caused any trouble, I was out. Growing up like that makes you think different, move different. That life teaches you how to protect yourself: you do what you have to do to survive. I never had a real family, and that's not meant to make anyone feel sorry for me but speaking my truth. There are others out there, I am sure, with their truths. I'm trying to make you understand that everything I do is to protect myself, and in doing so, it may hurt others. And because of that, I will forever be sorry."

I would like to believe the parents of these young people are doing the best they can with what they know. We know from our history the socio-economic status, bondage, and trauma of black and brown people in this country is traced back to slavery. We know there is a trickle-down effect, which was created to continue holding black and brown folks to a lower level and always maintaining some form of power over them. We know the history of oppression by those who considered black and brown less than human. And we know the systems they built so they could feel significant and beholden of power. What did not trickle down as much is the strong-willed mind of our ancestors, who knew that their mind was their weapon. They knew how to come together and think strategically on how to escape? We do stand on the shoulders of greatness, courage, boldness and strength. That can only be exhibited when everyone works on that "inner man." Because there is a long history of self-hatred and trauma within these blood lines, we know that it lends to the continued generational cycle of inward affliction and affixation on discontent for oneself and life. They are incapable of showing something to another human being if they have not experienced it for themselves.

Jesus reminds us that when you have 99 sheep, does the shepherd leave them to go after the one that has gone astray? The answer is yes. Because of what I see, I am reminded of how crucial love is and how necessary it is for us to function. God gave Moses the 10 commandments after He had noticed how self-absorbed His people had become. In all of the commandments, and throughout the Bible, God only asks us for two things -- TWO THINGS! He has asked us to love Him with all of our heart, with all of our mind, and with ALL of our soul. The next is to love our neighbor as we love ourselves. Here is where it gets challenging, and personally I can relate to my young people's struggle. It is hard to love others when you do not love yourself. Love can be distorted and shaped by an individual's environment. What I have appreciated about the young men I have worked with is their ability to express themselves in writing. It's writing they only do when isolated from the rest of the world because the noise in their normal environment is so loud it's deafening and the voices drown within them.

Children of the Fire/Flame

A life much better than this? The devils a liar
My parents never got married so I was born into the fire
I'm a stranger to faith, and unfamiliar with HOPE
I shed so much blood and tears the cloth I'm cut from is soaked.

I hear my stomach growling, I'm so hungry for a meal
My single mothers in her room bawling, I hope her wounds heal.
Our pain is identical but it's not quite the same
But no doubt in my mind, we're both children of the flame.

The children of the flame are dying out slowly
On the corners of the ghetto where the lands are unholy
But please understand we're born to lose and built to win
Because when you're born into the fire, you're born into sin.

And when most of my young people feel this way, but don't have the words to articulate what they feel, there cannot be any expectation of generational love until we begin to break it with one first.

CHAPTER 4

The Contradiction

As a mother of a young boy, my heart at times cannot be at rest. I see how the enemy has created the dissensions and divide within our world in order to build his army. God warns us of this, to not be of dissensions, envy, greed, power, and hate, which are everything our young ones are filled with. How do we bring them into what our spirit must be, which is one of love, kindness, hope, forbearance, peace, gentleness, and patience?

When my son was born, April 21, 2010, I began to look at the world differently and fearfully. My son was planned. He was not an accident. God knew he was coming, and so did I. Parts of me felt selfish because here is this life, fully dependent on me, and I am bringing him into a world that will tear him at every opportunity. God said before you were formed in your mother's womb, He knew you, He called you. Before my son was born, I began preparing for him. I wanted to make sure his life was as stable as possible. That he would not want for anything, and that his father and I were able to provide more than just a good home and safe environment, that we were ready to love someone more than ourselves. But I knew the world was filled with an evil I could not protect him from, enemies that would come after him because of who he was. I don't mean because he was a young man of color, but because more than anything, I was raising a man of God who happens to be of color. I believe those are the ones who are attacked the most.

The only thing I can give my son is Christ. Build him in God's Word, love, and to know who he is and his royal lineage. One day, I will not be here, but I need him to know that no matter what, he is protected; that the calling and anointing on his life is bigger, stronger, and more powerful than anything his father and I could ever give him. I will not be in the classroom when his peers question him or try to change him. I will not be in the school when adults look at him as another statistic or profile him. I will not be in the community or streets where those around him will try to influence him. I will be in the home and in the church, reminding him day in and day out of his divine destiny and purpose. I will build him alongside our Heavenly Father to run the race that has been marked out for him. When he gets tired, and he is ready to quit, I will be there cheering him on and reminding him that he can do this. No matter how many times he may stumble, fall, or go down a path that was not his, I will be there to love him and help him find his way back.

Our young people are not fighting "against flesh and blood, but against spiritual warfare, against the rulers, against the authorities, against the powers of this dark world and against the spiritual forces of evil in the heavenly realm" (Ephesians 6:12 NIV). This Scripture tells us clearly that our battle is not against people and what we can physically see. It's what we can't see that is our biggest threat. I am one mother, who has some but not all insight into what it will take to raise my son and now my daughter, but how many parents out there are able to do this? To pray without ceasing and to build them in truth? And can we fault them for not having the capacity to do so? How do we raise the next generation of God's warriors who are ready and equipped for battle?

One young man used the analogy that "it's like there is a two-headed snake within me." They want to make it; they want to be different, but at the same time, they don't want to be alone. The statistics are not carrying enough of them to the other side, and when almost all are on the negative side, it's easy for them to be complacent. Our young men are at war with each other, killing one another, taking a life with their own hands and losing theirs in the same grip. They will tell you that they are not afraid to die. That is the messaging they are passing on to their siblings, friends, peers, or worse, their kids -- that is not building a generation for God's kingdom, but one for the enemy. Each generation is losing more and more hope. They are fighting numb, and that is not who we are created to be.

Adults are quick to say that is the tough part of them speaking. The part that wants to make it seem as if they are not scared of anything. But the horror of that statement is accurate -- they are NOT afraid to die. What frightens them more than anything is to live. Living means being in the world and facing the demons and enemy, not the ones they are fighting, but the ones within themselves they can't control. These young men and women have not been taught the truth about war, how to fight and win. They have not been taught where the battle is and the real weapon used to win any and all battles. They are not in a fair place, and the enemy knows this. They are suiting up each day in the wrong armor. The colors they wear, the attire they see as necessary to keep in line, the sneakers, the hats, the jewelry: they believe that tells and shows who they are.

The enemy manipulates and takes our young men. He distorts the truths, and makes them believe they have to take power to be significant; that they have to have power to have those around them fear them because society does anyway. The enemy is smart; he plays upon their circumstances, against the things that have gone wrong, and against people who have come and gone in their life. He uses the notion, "If there was a God, where was He to allow all this to happen?"

I have heard young people several times ask if there is to be a "God" who is so mighty and controls all things, why do bad things happen? Why do good people die, why do children get sick, why do children go through abuse and sexual assault? If God were to exist, where is He when all of this happens? I have learned to let them ask those questions, but I do not pretend to have an answer. For any young person or individual of any age who is not rooted in Christ or knows

His essence, it is hard to fathom how He can love me yet allow bad things to happen.

The explanation I give is this. God does allow things to happen, and He ordains things to pass, and although we will never understand in this lifetime why, He has a greater purpose for it. Our life is not for us, but for someone else. What happens in it is meant to save someone else. In the beginning, God gave humans dominion over the sea and everything in it, over the land and everything that crawls/walks it. He gave us free will and choice. Things that have happened are a result of those who have claimed dominion and used it outside of the will and purpose of God. The evil we experience is a result of that, not that of God.

Understand that because we are human, we will make mistakes and take it upon ourselves to determine our path. When we choose our own path, it has consequences that are not necessarily ordained by God but allowed because He gave us the right to make choices. Our Father sees the final picture, something we do not have the privilege of knowing. Because we make choices, we bear the consequences of them. However, when we ask for His help and forgiveness, He will work out our mistakes for our good. There will be a blessing from our suffering, and although some cannot begin to understand that, trusting in Him and who He is is where our faith needs to take hold. Not everything in our life will be explained, and we have to learn that. He tells us to walk by faith and not by sight. Our faith produces the fruits and blessings, but, most importantly, Him in our life.

We want answers and explanations for things, though at times there will be none. But I ask: What harm could come from believing in Him? He is not asking you to kill, destroy, or hurt anyone. Rather He is saying to love each person, forgive him or her because they are not of their own doing, and offer grace to those who need it. He wants us to have a heart for love, compassion, and wisdom that He will graciously give us if we ask for it. We cannot forgive or love those who have hurt us in our own strength. We need to do it through His strength for the love and forgiveness that we need to bestow upon those who have hurt or wronged us.

As I look at our young people, my heart breaks because their lives are incomplete. They have gone from childhood to adulthood in a course of 12 years instead of 18 to 21, with no in-between. They missed the middle years where they were allowed to be carefree, to be stress free, to not know what it is like to worry about safety, food, warmth, and life. The path for us within this country has always had trials and challenges, some difficult and some gruesome, but it was not of our choosing to endure a life such as that. It was one that was given to people of color because of the evil that manifests within humans. The battle that ensues within our boys is one of systemic and oppressive choosing. They are not making it to adolescence, a period where they can challenge their thinking and decide what it is in life they want to become or where they would like to go. They are missing those critical phases in life and not reaching adulthood milestones. They are dying before the age of 21, and because they are so busy avenging someone's death they consider to be friend or family, it means they are not giving any consideration to their own future. They are not able to see the long-term plans and purpose because they are simply living in the here and now. They do not know how to see the future and have not been taught what hope is and how to hold on to it.

Our society is failing our young people in countless ways. Although we live in a country that allows us to worship as we see fit, it does not give us the creative freedom to give those who do not know Christ the option to ask and learn. Our churches welcome all, but they do not move beyond their walls for our young people. They are not the ones walking through the door in a time of crisis; their families are not bringing them, so how do we get to them? How do we reach these souls to teach them to fight the right way? It took me until the age of 32 to learn how to fight. To learn His words and His truths to sit on. In my darkest of days, one of His promises I hold to is Jeremiah 29:11 (NIV): "'For I know the plans I have for you,' declares the Lord, 'plans to prosper you and not to harm you, plans to give you hope and a future.'" This is my helmet when I am preparing for a battle. No matter what, I know God has allowed this battle in order to build me.

"The thief comes only to steal, kill and destroy; I have come that they may have life, and have life to the full" (John 10:10 NIV). That is my belt of truth. When I feel things beginning to tighten around me, I hold to this truth because I know it's a game that the other side is trying to use to distract me and throw me off my course. "For God so loved the world that he gave his one and only son, that whoever believes in him shall not perish but have eternal life" (John 3:16 NIV) is what I stand on as I strap on my boots to stand firm and know that He is right alongside me. "I can do all things through Christ who strengthens me" (Philippians 4:13 NKJV) is my breastplate strapped to my chest and dwells in my heart because He has already declared me victorious. My weapon, my sword that I use when I head into battle is this: "The Lord will fight for you; you need only to be still" (Exodus 14:14 NIV). The Lord is my sword because He reminds us that the battle is not ours, but His to fight. That we cannot win on our own, that our strength comes from Him, and our weakness is made perfect in Him. If we would only be still, trust in Him, and believe in Him, He will fight our battles, vindicate our injustices, and take care of our enemies.

As I think of His ultimate display of love for us, by giving us His son, I begin to become overwhelmed with emotions. As we have read, watched, and, even acted out Jesus's last days, He shows us how human He was. Jesus, who was perfect and blameless in every way, asked and pleaded with His Father not to let Him undergo the crucifixion. He asked Him to take away the cross. Now, as a parent, I could never imagine having to make that decision, to hurt one who did nothing wrong to save all who are wrong. It is why we are not capable of choosing who lives and who dies. So, when will we as a society take a stand on what is right and wrong?

When will we hold firm to the truth and stop passing judgment on our young ones, and start loving them the way they were meant to be loved so they could live?

Forgiveness is one of the hardest things to do. From friends to family to colleagues and those I have been in a personal relationship with, learning to forgive them was something that was not easy for me to do. I have encountered many forms of hurt from these people, ones that were meant to tear me and leave me helpless and hopeless. I found that carrying the anger in me was doing more damage to me than the person who had wronged me. You see, those people do not tend to think about their ways and their actions very often, so they do not see the pain and damage they have caused. But I (we) tend to carry it day in and day out. We tend to replay the situations over and over in our heads. We are the ones who put up walls and barriers for the next individuals who come in our life, assuming the next person is going to be the same way. We have unwillingness to trust, and because we do that, we lose that person. A person who had done nothing wrong, but because we are blinded by the pain and hurt of our past, we were not able to see them clearly for who they were and what they brought with them because we carried baggage from the past.

When Jesus explains that forgiveness is not for the other person, but for us, there is a reason He is explaining this truth to us. It is the only way we are free from that person. If not, we carry that person with us and give them power over us. It's hard to express that in the midst of the betrayal and hurt, but if our young ones learn what forgiveness is and see adults who are able to model forgiveness for them, they will begin to understand.

That is not the easiest thing to do. Remembering that my kids are watching me and the choices I make, but mostly, how they view the world through how I move throughout the world is a heavy weight to carry. My daughter has told me, "I am watching how you are loving yourself." Well, talk about pressure! But in the same breath, I am proud of her because she holds me accountable. I cannot expect her to demonstrate a love and compassion for others that she does not have for herself. I am able to be more forthcoming with her than my son, partly because of his age, but also because of gender. The weight of the world typically falls on women to be warriors, nurturers, and the glue that holds the family and everyone together. The woman is to help build her partner, but all while persevering in her own dreams. Proverbs 31:10-31, describes this woman as noble. "She is clothed in strength and dignity; / she can laugh at days to come. / She speaks with wisdom, / and faithful instruction is on her tongue" (v 25-26). The Bible describes this woman as being able to do it all because she reveres God. Women and men have always been held to a different standard.

In Lee Strobel's quest to prove Christianity is false, he fell upon many truths that I believe resonate with many young men, especially those of color. He made the connection between those who are non-believers and their fathers' wounds. It was pointed out that many significant historical figures such as Sigmund Freud, Friendrich Bietzsche, and others all had estranged or nonexistent relationships with their fathers that caused disbelief that there could be a God who is a heavenly, all-loving, caring and compassionate being who loves us unconditionally. The reality is because we as humans tend to believe and feel what we see, rather than hold to what the truth holds, if the feeling of abandonment, neglect, coldness, no affirmation and distance is all that some young men of color know, how could they possibly believe and have faith in a being that they cannot see? The father wounds for our young men are real, they are painful, and they dictate the decisions they make. The devil knows this, and if he can keep the generational loss of fathers continual by using and manipulating societal norms, then we keep the fatherless cycle going. Our country is experiencing an epidemic that no one talks about: More than 24 million children are without a father in the home. It has been predicted that number will continue to increase as we continue to experience younger generations of adolescents giving birth. It is alarming that we live in a country that is progressive, yet the idea that more than 24 million children are growing up with an absent parent continues to show how far removed we are from the church.

Having young men grow into adult men without a male figure present in the home is a disadvantage because they are not making the connections of what it is to be a man -- to walk like a man, to talk like a man, and to love like a man. If there is a male figure in the home, whether it be through an older brother, a boyfriend of Mom's, a relative or close friend to the family, how many of those men are Christ minded? They are not growing in knowing themselves because half of who created them is absent. They also are not being given the full picture of knowing they're royalty, that there is a Heavenly Father waiting for them who wants to know them and for them to get to know Him. What they are hearing from the adult raising them is more negative than positive about the father who is not in their life. For everyone negative that a child or person hears, it takes the counter of seven positives to negate that damage. Because they are being raised by individuals who are hurting themselves, the constant reminder of their flaws and comparison to a father they do not know is something that is a constant and a reality for these boys.

I remember a conversation with a mother of one of my young men. She said her son was a failure just like his father. How his father had said he was going to do all these great things with his life and attend Ben Franklin, but he never made it. I was a stranger, but she was willing to tell of her son's failure and his lack of abilities. I wonder what message she was giving to him.

But He tells us to love our enemies and to pray for those who do wrong against us because we cannot claim to love Him, who we don't see, and hate those we do see. Forgiveness is the hardest act for most humans to express. In a world where parents think of themselves first, we tend to raise children with that same mindset. We tend to look at how we have been wronged, at those who have mistreated us, how we have been abused and neglected. We feel the abandonment and betrayal we have encountered by those we love, the hurt and pain -- physical and mental -- we have suffered. We keep a tight hold of all that pain as if it's our protection. When we re-live the pain, forgiveness is the furthest thing from our minds because the strength of the emotion continues to ignite at the thought of it. When one understands forgiveness and how to let go, they then understand it is a process. As I had to learn to forgive those who have hurt me in countless ways, it never dawned on me that it was a repetitive action. You do not realize that you have to forgive continuously to ease the pain because the memories may remain. He tells us that our fight is not against flesh and blood, but against the spirits we do not see. People are inherently corrupt and evil and we are all by nature wicked, but the mind has altered its beliefs to fulfill one's own desires.

We often see our young people as damaged, and they, in turn, begin to see themselves that way. It begins to grow within their spirit and it shapes how they see themselves. They become broken men who are desperate to seek someone to fix them, to fix what they believe is incomplete or missing from their lives. They cling to the slightest bit of attention and mistake it for love. They confuse it with a treatment they are used to, but it has disguised itself in a different form. Our boys of color have grown in a world that continues to label and depict their trajectory and allows those negative beliefs to play in their heads. They continue to see themselves as less than, growing into men who are bitter and hold resentment for never feeling like they could rise to more.

As I listen to my young people sitting in khaki slacks, white t-shirts, and navy blue sweaters in the detention facilities, I hear the anguish and confusion in their tone. They speak of their families and the chaos that ensues in their household. Of how their families fight among each other -- verbally and physically -- and lay blame on one another for the negativity in their lives. Many of these young men are being raised by women who have been torn, beaten, and bruised and are shamed by their iniquities. Because of that, women are raising their children in pain that is manifested into the growth and development of young people and leaving their souls empty and filled with a distorted depiction of love. The enemy knows how to divide, and he has been successful at that in the black and brown communities. From our homes to our communities to education and to our professional ambitions, the divide is heavily embedded within dissentions of our people who are challenged with building among us or believing the lies that as a group we are not all able to rise.

The strength of women has changed over the course of time. Women have given our crowns, our rightful heir, to men who have no understanding of how to treat us. We seek their love and attention, their affirmation, their strength, because they are supposed to be our partners. They are supposed to be our protection, and I do not mean just in the physical sense, but in every facet of safety. Often the confusion lies in the word submission that is used in the Ephesians 5, which says wives are to be submissive to their husbands. Here is where we do not read carefully, or choose not to acknowledge, that God says husbands are to treat their wives like Christ treated the church (Ephesians 5:25).

We quote 1 Corinthians 13 over and over again, to the point that it has lost its value in meaning. "Love is patient, love is kind. It does not envy, it does not boast, it is not proud. It does not dishonor others, it is not self-seeking, it is not easily angered, it keeps no record of wrongs" (v 4-5). But how quick are we to deflect on others, how quick we are to bring up a hurt someone has caused or to boast about our accolades and ourselves. We continue to demonstrate false appreciation for others when in reality we feel as if we deserve better or what they have. We are self-seeking when we can't hold accountability for our actions, for words that come out of our mouths and tear someone else down. We drive past a homeless person or make accusations as to how that person ended up on drugs or living on the streets. We are ALL guilty of this, but yet we are so eager to quote in reference to a new love. This verse is meant more than just as a gesture of love in a romantic relationship, but as how Christ loved us as His children, as His sisters and brothers, but more importantly, how we are to love each relationship within our life.

I am not here to distinguish that we all settle for less than we deserve, both men and women. Because of this downfall, it gets passed on to our children, and they can only grow in what they see and what they know. The contradiction that lies within what we tell ourselves, the lies the enemy has built within this society, and the battle for the truth God has given to those who will believe. The truth He has given us, 2 Chronicles 7:14 KJV if those who are called by name shall humble themselves, and pray, and seek my face, and turn from their wicked ways, then I will hear from heaven, and will forgive their sin, and will heal their land." He can and will restore us.

CHAPTER 5

The Hope and Purpose Within

As I reflect on my life, I will admit there were times I doubted, lost hope, and had no faith in God. Most of the time we learn the surface level of who God is and the basics of what religion is. It wasn't until I began to feel the gap in my life widen and deepen that I knew something was missing. It took time for me to learn that it was not something missing but someone missing in my life. That hole then drew me into the beginning stages of my relationship with Christ.

There is a difference in the way we understand Christ and His purpose for us. Going to church and half-heartedly listening to a message being preached does not fill you. Once you begin to seek God, you learn the difference between religion and relationship. Jesus did not come and die for us to play religion. God did not send His only son for us to go to a building once a week and listen to someone read from a Bible. Jesus came for much more than that. When you read of Him in Scripture, He demonstrates that what He desires and wants from us is a relationship. He wants to get to know us and for us to choose to tell Him about us. He already knows all there is to know about us and where we are going, every mistake we have made or will make. He desires a deep personal and intimate connection with us in which we are choosing to come to Him with all the details of our lives because He is the only one who could help us steer and navigate the circumstances in our lives. I had to lay down everything before Him. My weaknesses, my sins, my fears, and the words of those that consume me.

I didn't understand Him or why He would die for me. I didn't understand why He would love me unconditionally for all the wrong and for all of the sin I had committed. I have not done much in my life that I regret, but that does not mean I am perfect. In fact, I am far from perfect. I have flaws, I have hurt people, and I am selfish—at the end of the day, I am human. I have learned to repent and ask for forgiveness and believe in the hope and truth He promises. I have learned over time to forgive myself for mistakes I have made and to be accountable for the role I play in other people's lives. That is not easy, and that takes time. I do not carry some of the darkness that many of these young people do. Who is going to tell them that they are forgiven through the blood of Jesus Christ, that their mistakes are not bigger than the love God has for them? If I felt this way—not having any understanding of who Christ was and why God loved me— how could I expect them to understand that the hope and love their Heavenly Father has for them eases the pain of their past and present? I have seen how far I have come, and I am excited for where He is leading me. It has taken me a while to get to this point, to know and understand that the pain, circumstances, struggles, and fear in my life will be used by Him for my good. I tell young people that He is preparing them for something amazing; they just have to hold on and believe. He cares and will not waste a single moment in your life, a single hurt, a single tear that you have shed. For His Word tells us that, "I will be glad and rejoice in your love / for you saw my affliction / and knew the anguish of my soul" (Psalm 31:7 NIV).

How do we define love? Each individual has his or her own way of defining love. By taking time to examine how we define love, we will then be able to begin to do the work needed for us to understand the love we were meant for and how we love ourselves. One of the most common reasons youth are in detention facilities is because they are seeking something they were not receiving in the comfort of their home or, most importantly, in themselves. Young people thrive on a relationship that builds them physically, mentally, emotionally, and spiritually. These young people do not have the correct vernacular to describe or articulate exactly what it is they are looking for, but the one message that is clear is this: they want someone who cares about them and listens to them.

The fears that echo through the unit on the detention center as I listen to my young people are these, "No one knows what it is we are walking in," and "I need to trust that person in order for me to talk about what I am going through." Love is a language they cannot express healthily because they have not been able to receive it or understand what it is supposed to look like. The relationships that are supposed to define love begin with our parents or guardians. As I began to look into the five love languages described by Gary Chapman, we can begin to understand that if we were never in a home or environment where we heard positive things about ourselves, heard loving words, or saw kindness and compassion, then we do not know how to give that in return to another person. Words of affirmation are where we as humans begin to define our value and how we feel about ourselves. However, if we never hear anything good about ourselves, we are not going to feel or believe anything positive. It creates the struggle of being able to communicate anything positive to others, which is evident by the relationships many of these young people have with adults and authority figures in their lives. They never learned how to treat them because the adults in their life did not know how to communicate love and respect to them. As one young man stated, "You grow up in this world and think that it is normal and that is what it is supposed to look like."

Jesus teaches us that love is meant to be unconditional. God came in human form, as Jesus Christ demonstrated to us what unconditional love is. Jesus, our compass, showed us how to navigate this world. Throughout the Bible, we are told about God's love for us and the expectation He has of His children. But if you do not know how much God loves you and why He loves you, it is impossible to love yourself, let alone anyone else. Each of us is a special creation of the Lord.

Jeremiah 1:5 (ESV) tells us so, "Before I formed you in the womb I knew you, / and before you were born I consecrated you; / I appointed you a prophet to the nations." As we begin to define love and discuss what it is, we have to realize that we are it. We are love because we are no accident.

In 2017, it became clear to me—from the workplace to the community that I worked in and the young people lived in—that how we see the children in front of us is an example of how much we value and devalue ourselves all at the same time. The world we currently live in is filled with emotionally unstable beings, and our children have suffered as a result of it. Society has allowed us to use power over our children in a manner that has left them feeling helpless, angry, and out of control.

Let me be clear on what I mean. Jesus told us what His Heavenly Father is looking for from us. I will continue to repeat this. We are to love God with all of our heart, mind, and soul, and next we are to love our neighbor as ourselves. The first one is clear, and most people are able to understand that. Whether they follow it is another question. We are to love God with every ounce of our being; nothing is to come before Him. Not our spouse/partner nor our children, certainly not our career/work, and, of course, not even us.

The second commandment is not clear although it may appear to be. We are to love our neighbor, which indicates everyone who comes into our life and path, as we love ourselves. Here is where I have found that it gets hard and where the questions in my head begin to come in. What if you do not know how to love yourself?

Most of us, including me, have a false sense of what love is. How I saw and expressed love was based on how I believed and saw love as I was growing up from my home, school, television, and from those around me. The truth is that is how most of us learn what love is growing up. We learned that love was conditional. When we did something good, we felt valued and appreciated. We got rewards, we were told positive things, we were even showcased. When we did something bad, we were punished, rejected, given negative comments and criticism, and disciplined.

I am not saying discipline is wrong. The Bible tells us that discipline is important and even God disciplines those He loves. Discipline is what makes us stand strong in who we are and in our convictions. Punishment is another story. Punishment and discipline have been intertwined and given the same definition when in reality they are different and need to be treated as such. Society has once distorted what is meant to build us rather than tear us down. We use punishment as an excuse for discipline without realizing the damage it has cost us until it is too late. This current generation of young people are the result of society's punishment on those they have labeled, judged, and condemned. Society just has not realized it yet. It will realize it when it's too late.

Young people are becoming blind with anger and rage. What is really going on is that one more person in their life is continuing to devalue them. When young people make the statement that they feel disrespected, what that is really saying to me is, "Yet again, someone is not listening to me." Young people from the beginning have been overlooked, under-appreciated, but, most importantly, they have not been built and loved in a way that fills them because they have been taught that it is conditional. How many parents disown a child when they hear that their son or daughter has married outside of their race or religion or married someone of the same sex? They shut them out of their lives because they do not agree with their choices. A person they carried within them for nine months? When we look at those around us who don't do well with managing the pressures and stresses of life, we see many who drink, smoke, inject, take pills, etc., all of which is a form of self-medication to numb the hurt and pain they feel and do not know what to do with, and that tells me a lot. What that shows is the inability to love themselves, and when we don't love ourselves, it is impossible to love someone else, including our own children. Whether they are our biological children, nieces, nephews, stepchildren, students, or any other young person put in our path, we love them as we love ourselves, on a conditional and temporary or moment by moment basis.

If you believe in Christ and follow His beliefs, you know that love is meant to be unconditional. God created us in His image, and His image is that of love. If the greatest commandment is to love God with all of our core, then we need to understand that we are made to need love. How we demonstrate it is what determines the success of those we love. When we acknowledge that words have power, and that they determine the path we will walk, we will begin to understand what we need, and more importantly, what our children need?

From my observation of some of the young men on the pretrial unit in one of the facilities that I have worked with, words are extremely impactful, and they have determined the trajectory for our young men. My fear and worry from my work is this: my young men do not know who they are, which leaves them feeling respondent to those who try to define them. From parents, legal guardians, teachers, and those in authority, society continues to tell us who we are. This is the danger that plagues our young people because they have not been grounded in whom they belong to and the royalty they are. They do not understand that they are more than their environment, that our Heavenly Father's love for them is unconditional and that the mistakes they have made do not define who they are or determine their future as long as they learn to trust in Him.

Words can build us up, and they can tear us down. He tells us the tongue is like a double-edged sword. He tells us that the tongue is deceitful. What others say about our character has the power to cut us deep because we begin to believe, and the enemy knows this. It is why his tactics start when we are young. The words and power they hold embedded from a young age, and he reminds us of those words, that pain. It is why it is so critical how we speak to our children. It doesn't go away. I would like you to take a moment and think of some of the words you heard when you were growing up. We hurt more when it is those closest to us. It begins to devalue and strip you from your identity.

Christ has told us over and over: Our Heavenly Father, who is the King of all high, has created us in His image to be a blessing. We are the princes and princesses of the Most High, and until that it is ingrained and woven into the fabric of our being, we will never settle into our destiny or purpose. When we can stand firm in who we are, we can walk intelligently in our ways. It won't matter what anyone says about us because we will not waver like the sea or question our worth. It is then our young men can stand boldly in their skin and walk in confidence that their future is promising -- as long as they continue to have hope and faith.

Over and over the Bible states that we are to watch what we say. We are to keep our lips guarded. We are to be slow to speak, slow to anger, and quick to hear. As we learn to love ourselves unconditionally, we can begin to dismantle the generational curses that plague our country, our children, and the generations to come. We continue to curse those who come after us when we do not stand tall and fight the giants currently in our life.

Saul did not conquer the Philistines when he had the opportunity to do so because fear held him prisoner. Rather, he stated that his children's battles were theirs to fight. However, they were not equipped to fight because he did not show them how. What we leave unturned in our present life, we risk and leave for our children. They watch, wait, and follow in our footsteps. When they do not have the courage to do differently, we get upset and, in many ways, blame them. However, the reality is that it was our failure that left them inept to begin with. Generation Y is an angry generation, and it's because we have left so many giants for them to fight. We have not equipped them, suited them, or prepared them, yet we expect them to win.

"They tried to bury us, but they did not know we were seeds."

CHAPTER 6

The Breaking

Jesus told us that the greatest commandment was to love His father with all of our heart, all of our mind, and all of our soul and next to love our neighbor as ourselves. What if you do not love yourself? If you do not love yourself, how do you love your neighbors/others? His Word tells us, "Love is patient, love is kind. It does not envy, it does not boast, it is not proud. It does not dishonor others, it is not self-seeking, it is not easily angered, it keeps no record of wrongs" (1 Corinthians 13:4-5 NIV). But the world that is full of people who are not able to love in that capacity because they are not able to love themselves in that manner.

As a woman of color living in a superficial society, it is hard to love what you see in the mirror when society embeds at a young age "perfection": the must-have, notoriety, money, physical and social image, and everything you pretty much are not unless you are born with a silver spoon and can acquire all of that. You become hard and critical of yourself in every way, from the way you look to the way you act to how you live and eventually into what you become. You begin to question if any of your goals are based on your own thoughts and desires for yourself, or what culture dictates you need to have and do in order to be happy?

Young people have built their happiness in a false world the enemy has created to continue his plight with the minds of those who are susceptible to believing they are not enough. Television, radio, and every other media outlet have convinced and raised the young people of this generation. The nature vs. nurture argument some can say is a challenge now more than ever. Besides worrying about peers and physical environment playing a role in the development of children, you have media that have produced more of an influence that sides and feeds the nurture debate of young people's development. Our world continues to influence young people, especially young black and brown boys and girls who are growing up prematurely because of misconceived, doctored, and pretentious realities.

This world calls people "broken" or that they come from "broken homes," without taking time to pay attention to the trajectory that has led these young people to where they are. Society has done a remarkable job at dictating who is and who isn't whole or normal without fully explaining what whole or normal means. Therefore, it creates the notion that if all things are not within a social construct, it is misplaced, abnormal, or broken. I denounce the thought that our young people are broken because that gives society too much power. No one should ever have that much power to determine who is or isn't normal or broken.

I have fallen prey to these same tactics that the enemy is using. The Bible warns us to guard our hearts, for everything you do flows from there. It warns us to be cautious about what we watch, what we hear, and what feeds into us. It does this because as humans we are susceptible to falling and allowing the enemy access into our most sacred inner core, our mind. In our mind is where thoughts are shaped, lies are told, false realities are made, and fear and doubt reside. When all that is formulated, we react, we respond, and we give life to it. By giving life to it, we have just now given the enemy reign and control over us.

I go back to the idea of loving ourselves. Again, if we cannot love ourselves, how do we love others around us? How do we love our children? We love based on how we were loved; we begin imparting on them what was imparted on us. The Old Testament talks about generational curses passed down, but do we really know what that means? When we speak of illnesses and traits passing from generation to generation, we never think about the inner unclean spirits that were never dealt with that are handed down as well.

The story of David and Goliath is a perfect example of generational curses. Goliath was a Philistine, one abnormal in size who used that abnormality to invoke fear and doubt in Israel. Based on his size, Saul's kingdom judged that they were no match for him, that they would not be able to win in war against him and his people. Saul, a king with tremendous power and wealth, could not get beyond his own insecurities and worry, so he allowed Goliath to reign fear over his people for quite some time. David had two older brothers who were in Saul's army and were angered when David would ask questions about Goliath. Because David's brothers were not able to defeat Goliath, it caused David, the youngest of Jesse's sons, to fight Goliath.

To give present context on what I mean, I will use myself and some of the young people I have worked with as an example. For as long as I can remember, I struggled with fear, worry, doubt, and anxiety. I did not want to make anyone upset or hurt anyone's feelings. Even if someone was causing me great distress and had set out to hurt me, it was hard for me to confront them. I was so insecure in who I was that I allowed others to make me feel less than rather than dealing with it.

From the age of five, I noticed the same qualities in my son. I have seen on the playground other children being mean to him or making snide comments to him, and he would look at them but not say anything. I could tell he knew that they were being mean to him, but he didn't stand up for himself. A mother never wants to see her child experience those moments; she wants to fight the battle for them. Now, I won't lie, although I did not say anything to the kids, I did say something to the parents. The one area of my life that I did not lose my voice is defending and fighting for my children. I do not mean just my own children, but all young people who have been placed before me. It is the one thing, as I mentioned earlier, that will send me into another being.

As my son continued to get older, I noticed that he was also this way with his father and me. As a divorced parent, you work hard to not have your children in the middle of anything because you never want them to feel as if they have to choose. His father and I, by the grace of God, have done ok in co-parenting. I would never say we were great or perfect at it because that would be a lie. We have had our stumbles along the way, but the one thing I can say for sure is that we both love our son more than anything. At times, we have had to sit back and think whether our decisions are about us or about him. We both have a great relationship with our son, but there are things we do differently that make him respond to us differently. With that being said, our son does not address things because he does not want to hurt our feelings. Again, as a mom, to see that same trait does not sit well.

Our young people watch everything we do. Words are strong, and they are powerful. They can cut or build any person. Actions followed by words are what make the impact. We cannot tell our kids to be strong, to be bold, or to believe and hope in things when we do not do the same. What we leave unturned in our present life, we risk leaving for our children. They watch, wait, and follow in our footsteps, and when they do not have the courage to do differently, we get upset and blame them. But it was our failure that left them inept to begin with. Generation Y is an angry generation, and it's because we have left so many giants for them to fight. We have not equipped them, suited them, or prepared them, yet we expect them to win. The ones to come after Generation Y will be worse if we do not change trajectories now. After the Millennials, the gap in the church's age group is glaringly obvious. Young people are not hearing the truth about who they are, who they were created to be or how loved they are.

We live in a world where the definition of words has lost value and meaning and is interpreted to fit the rationalization of those using it. Love is a word that is used loosely, thrown around cavalierly, and used for personal agenda rather than in truth. Biblical love is truth; the biblical definition clarifies the various meanings of love. The kind of love that God wants us to have is what He calls "agape," love that is unconditional. It is the kind of love I believe EVERY HUMAN yearns for. It's the kind of love I desire. When your heart and core desire that kind of love, you will attempt to find it everywhere and anywhere. If you desire that type of love, you can become lost trying to find it. Looking for that love and finding things or people to fill it can become intoxicating.

This new generation is being raised in the age of social media, digital imaging, and image/body distortion, the idea that you have to change the way you look to be loved. Young girls are constantly seeing images of what the "ideal sexy woman" should look like, and if you do not look like that, there are a lot of ways to get that look, from injections and chemicals, to surgery and ingesting pills. All that comes at a cost, financially, mentally, and emotionally. How are we combatting those tactics by the enemy?

For men, it's what you need to have in order to get an "ideal woman" or to have a life of notoriety. It is also glamorizing what relationships look like. Treating a woman as property, trophy, status, and as less than an equal is an idea that has become popular and relevant in today's culture. What folks do not realize is that, because of all this, it makes young people believe that if they do not look like this, act this way, or have any of these things, something is wrong. It's giving credence to idolatry. Idolizing a look/image is no different than historical times when people worshipped idols/statutes.

We have our own interpretation of what "broken" means, and in this particular chapter, I share my definition of broken. As I share more personal stories on my walk, this chapter holds me accountable while at the same time exposing my weaknesses, insecurities, and the truth. My for doing this is so you can see what is in front of you and know the needs of these young people. To do that, you have to have a biblical foundation of what "broken" is in order to know what healing and deliverance are. Throughout the chapters, I have given reference to my walk, my experiences, and the work I have been created to do. But in this chapter, I speak about my connection and relationship with God, rather than the religion I played along with.

Most of my life, I considered myself to be a good person—a good person with flaws like every other human. I get upset over things that some view as minor; I can hold a grudge when someone offends me or when I feel wronged. I can be petty and "remind" people of their shortcomings. I am even good at letting you have it and cutting you at the knees without you even realizing that I am doing so. Again, flawed like every other human—and I am sure most of you, if you are honest, might realize you have some of the same flaws. That is not where I consider myself to be a good person; that was just me sharing in my humanity with you.

I believe I shared with you in the beginning of this book my "why" and believing I knew everything and I could solve everything. I also hinted that I still believe I am superwoman and can save the world. Well, here is where I tell His truth about me. In the beginning of this chapter, I spoke about "breaking" and being "broken." Most people use the term to describe that they are "broken" or a person is "broken." Some make statements that they have reached their "breaking" point. What I share is what I believe is the true definition of "broken." To me, the only person who can break you is the one who created you. There is nothing like being broken by God, especially when you don't see it coming.

Two years ago, April 11, 2018, I was in a car accident that I should not have been able to walk away from. The injuries I suffered were mild compared to what should have been the outcome. Again, before I dive more into that, let me back up a little and share in my mindset and outlook on life in order for you to understand the significance of the car accident. Before you assume, "Oh like most, you had a near-death experience or life-altering experience to have a 'come to Jesus' moment," this isn't quite like that.

In 2018, Easter was Sunday, April 1, meaning Holy Week was the week of March 25 through the 31. I tell you this so you have a timeline of events that occurred that week in my life. Every year, my church does an amazing Easter play production, which I regularly attend—even if I have seen it several times. Although we know what Christ suffered for us to be where we are and we are redeemed, we often need reminding—at least I do. I attended that year by myself, and as usual, I went into the church, made minimum contact with folks, and sat in my usual seat. The associate pastors were greeting folks as they arrived and meeting those invited, and the senior pastor, who makes it a point to shake hands with everyone, was making his rounds.

I have to share the fact that I LOVE MY CHURCH. Most folks say that about their home church, and just how amazing it is, so, yes, I am one of those people. I think the world of my senior pastor and his team. As my senior pastor made his way around, he stopped where I sat, gave me a hug hello, and asked me how I was doing. I kept it short and told him I was doing ok, which was far from the truth.

The truth was that I was at a low point in my life. Work had gotten to a point where I felt attacked from every angle. Not by the darkness of the work itself and trying to encourage young people who were incarcerated to stay hopeful, to create roadmaps for their lives, and to be willing to give themselves a chance by understanding that everything happens for a reason and to write their story. That was hard, but it wasn't what plagued me, made me cry each and every day, or consider if I was where I was supposed to be. I had heard in a sermon once by Bishop T.D. Jakes (another person I have much admiration for) that you could be in a place where you are skilled and talented, but it does not mean it's your purpose.

At that point in that Easter Holy Week, I was wondering if I was in the right place because if I was, why did it feel so unbearable? You see, what they do not tell you before you work in education is about all of the politics, the conniving tactics, undermining, and selfishness that actually happen when decisions are being made in regard to the lives of young people. I had been tasked with understanding the needs of young people who were court/system-involved and creating opportunities for them. Working toward eliminating barriers that often are placed before these particular young people because of the perception, stigma, and stereotypes that occur. Working to create pathways for young people with these sets of challenges is not easy on any level.

It wasn't that the young people were the challenge, though you would think they were. It was the adults who had the power to open doors, create change, and grant opportunities. Even though they did not want to work to help, I did not understand why they wanted to prevent me from doing so. As a young black woman, I had challenges already before me working and surviving in a white-male dominated world. However, now the challenges presented from all angles, and I could not understand why. I will not dwell on all that occurred in the three years I worked in that position, but I will tell you, I felt pressed on every side. This was around the time T.D. Jakes' book *Crushed* was released, and I had just about given up hope and was ready to walk away from it all. I had worked long hours, sometimes seven days straight, to figure out how to bring hope and opportunities to these young people that so many wanted to keep down and out of sight.

I was tired of fighting; I was mentally and emotionally exhausted; I felt lost. That is the mindset I was in when my pastor approached me at the Easter play. As he began to walk away, he stopped and stood still for a minute, and then he turned around and came back to me. He said to me, "I am teaching a new class this Wednesday called the Emotionally Healthy Leader, and I really think you should join."

I looked at him and smiled. I said, "I think it sounds like what I need," and agreed that I would be there. I sat down and thanked God for hearing me. God tells us His ways are not our ways, and His thoughts are higher than our thoughts (see Isaiah 55:8-9). I mention this because I thought this is where my help, the direction, the clarity I needed would come from. Maybe it was time for me to leave or figure out if I was the leader that I was meant to be. I knew I had a lot of issues, and this course would allow me to process if it was me or if it was something else and how to fix it.

The first class began that Wednesday, April 5. I showed up; I had purchased the book but had not read it yet. I sat down and waited for class to begin. One of the very first things my pastor said was, "If you are not ready to do some real work, you are not ready for this class." I thought to myself, *Hmm, ok, this is going to be interesting.* Little did I know. He spoke about how this class was going to really expose who you are. Again, I thought to myself, *What does that mean?* We went through introductions, spoke a little about ourselves and why we were there. I remember my statement was more on whether I was a leader, and if I were to become one, this would help. So, what is interesting about what I said is that because I did not have a title that would particularly distinguish me as a leader, I had let societal norms dictate and convince me that I was not a leader and that I was not enough to be one. I remember my pastor giving me a somewhat quizzical look, but he did not ask me to go further in my statement.

I left that evening feeling as if I were in the right place taking this class, and I could not wait until the following week to learn more. I also had to do the reading beforehand; I just needed to find the time. My life consisted of a 90-minute drive to work; work until about five most days; and at least a 90-minute drive back home. When I got home, it was checking my son's homework, making sure he had eaten dinner, discussing his day and school, if he was not in sports at the moment. Then it was getting him ready for the next day, making his lunch, getting his clothes ready, making sure he took his bath, reading before bed, and prayers before bed. This is all typical of most parents who work and are single.

After he was all set, it was time for me to get myself together and then, usually, back on the computer doing work until I fell asleep. Wake up the next day, and do it all over again.

On the weekends, my son was usually with his father, and you would think I would use that time to rest. Nope, I spent the weekends going to the Department of Youth Services to hang out with the kids, play basketball, play games, and I had started a book club as well as teaching a curriculum I had created when I was a high school teacher. I did, however, attend church every Sunday: I never missed a service unless I was extremely sick, and I still don't. It was the one place I went where I felt all was right with the world. For those 75 minutes, I did not have to think, I did not have to worry, I did not have to talk, fight, or do anything. I was in my Father's house, and I could just sit and be His child.

Back to April 11, 2018. I left work and was driving home; traffic was actually moving at a steady pace, which was surprising. My car has Bluetooth, so I was not holding the cell phone as I called my mom. I had just entered the tunnel, and my mother had picked up. I told her I was on my way home, and she said ok. As soon as she said ok, the call dropped. Now, I drive the same way to work and home from work each day; I know where the dead spots are, and this was not a dead spot.

As soon as the call dropped, the car in front of me slammed on the brakes. I immediately slammed on mine. I looked in my rearview mirror, and the car behind me—well, he did not stop. At full speed, he slammed right into me. My head hit the steering wheel and the head rest. After realizing what happened, I was positive I had to have hit the car in front of me because I was less than an inch from it when I slammed on the brakes. But I hadn't. The car in front of me was gone.

But I couldn't move. I was dizzy, and the other driver's car was stuck in the trunk of my SUV. I called the police and let them know what was going on and then called my mother. I remember telling her to go into another room because I did not want my son to hear the conversation. I told her what happened and that I did not know what was going to happen because I was not sure of my injuries at the time besides my head feeling like a brick and I couldn't see or really think. The police and ambulance came. I remember thinking to myself, *I have never been in an ambulance before; this is a strange experience.*

I got to the hospital, but I am not sure how long I was there. I remember them asking about my head, taking X-rays and an MRI. They kept asking me if anything hurt and if I could move everything. I am pretty sure I could because they let me go home that evening. They reported nothing was broken, but I had a concussion and I would be more aware of what was bothering me the next day. In the meantime, I had to refrain from light, technology, and sudden movements, and I needed brain rest. I don't know if I physically did, but I know part of me thought they were crazy: what in the world was brain rest? I did not know what happened to my car. The police report was apparently given to me while at the hospital, but it was put in my bag. I do remember going home, explaining in some fashion to my son what happened—of course, doing my best not to alarm him—taking off my clothes, and going to bed.

In the middle of the night is when everything hit me—the pain, and I could not move the right side of my body, including lifting my neck from the pillow. I remember feeling around for my cell phone, calling my mom, and telling her she needed to come into my room. I thought I couldn't move. I started panicking: did they miss something at the hospital? This wasn't whiplash; I had been in a minor accident before and rear ended, but this was no body ache. I really couldn't move.

My mom lifted me into a sitting position, but the light was on next to my bed, and it was making me feel worse, so she had to put the light on in my bathroom in order to see to help me. She got the prescription that had somehow gotten filled. I took the pills and just sat there until it began to kick in. It felt like forever before it did, and I just remember sitting there in the dark with just the light from my bathroom and thinking, *What is this? What is going on right now? I do not have time to be out of it.*

I must have fallen asleep because I just remember the next morning my son coming into the room to say goodbye as he was leaving for school. He leaned over, gave me a kiss and asked how I was feeling. Of course, I said, "Fine. Momma's head just hurts a little." I was afraid to even try moving and have him notice something was wrong. My son is very observant, very sensitive, and very protective of me. His dad was outside waiting for him, and he left. I laid there for a moment not sure what I was able to do. I remember that I tried to use my legs to turn me over, but I was not having much luck on my right side. I was able to roll to my left and slowly—and I do mean slowly—get myself to sit, but I could not really move my neck, and my right shoulder was just not functioning. I went through that first day in pain and confused, and I do not mean just physically, but mentally and emotionally.

I called my supervisor that day to let him know that I was in a car accident. I told him about my physical condition and how I needed to be out for a minimum of two weeks because of the concussion, not being able to drive, etc. I had believed I was really close to my boss, since I had been a major support to him when he first moved to the city. I was a friend and comforter through his trials and tribulations, both personally and professionally. I have always been protective of him, considering those around him only pretended to appreciate him. So, understand why I would be completely hurt when he was less than compassionate during my accident. He simply acknowledged what I was saying and said to check in. I got off the phone completely torn by the conversation. I told my mother about it and how the last few months I had felt a disconnect between him and me. The once supportive, caring boss I had was no longer, and he had become a short, closed off, and distant man who barely had time to check in with me around my work.

I continued to lay in bed and felt even more isolated. I remained in bed the entire day, taking the muscle relaxers and Motrin for pain as needed. Pain killers make my stomach turn, so I tend to stay away from those. My mind kept thinking about work and people at work, things I needed to do: summer was around the corner and I needed to get the program ready; the superintendent was expecting my presentation on the work I had done the past year—all these things just kept spinning around. My mind would not stop, and it was 1 a.m., so I had decided to begin reading the book for church, *The Emotionally Healthy Leader*. I just needed something to distract me and take my mind off of things. Well, thirty minutes into reading, I figured out what my pastor meant about being ready to take this class. It completely tore apart everything I thought I knew about being healthy and being a leader. Two different concepts that are contingent upon one another.

I shut the book, and said to myself, *Well, I guess that explains a lot.* When Peter Scazzero makes the statement in describing attributes of an unhealthy leader, "they do more activity for God than their relationship can sustain for God" hit me pretty hard. The busyness of life, the "too much to do in too little of time" resonated because it was my constant. I did not take time to rest; I was constantly overextending myself, not just with work, but with always wanting to be there for others—even at the risk of my health and well-being. I fell asleep, now questioning myself rather than thinking over the trivial things that were plaguing me prior to reading.

I awoke the next morning to my son coming into my room again, letting me know he was leaving for school and would be with Daddy for the weekend. I gave him a kiss and a hug, let him know how much I loved him, and thanked him for being so awesome while Mommy was not feeling well. As he left, I looked at the clock on my cable box, 7:30 a.m., and I stared at my ceiling thinking about my day: I had a doctor's appointment at 3 p.m. I adjusted myself to go back to sleep, and as I did—He came.

I lay in my bed frozen, eyes closed, as He began to speak to me. He showed me visions of the last several years of my life, how He was shaping me with every job I had, how He had been preparing me all along the way. I could hear Him clearly ask me several times, "Why do you doubt?" For 15 minutes, God showed me all the areas where I had gone wrong. Even though the work I did was good work, I did them with wrong motives and did them in my own strength. I did not come to Him with my work, and although He had gifted me with certain skills and abilities, He was not at the forefront of it. I carried it all myself because I thought I could do it all myself. He also reminded me I was where I was supposed to be. After 15 minutes of revelation, I opened my eyes with tears, thanked Him, and asked for His forgiveness.

Without going into all of it, what I want you to understand is that the world telling you who you are and God showing you His preparation in you are vastly different things. But also, God humbling you is another form of breaking. You can lie to yourself and convince yourself of the "good" you think you are doing, but if He isn't in the center of it, it's not as good as you think it is.

My young men who were either in juvenile facilities or adult prison have spoken to me about the unbelief in God, the lack of trust they have within their family, and that the connection they felt and built were with the ones who they believed to be quite like them. I listened as some of them spoke about seeing family killed at the age of 8 and the wall it built within them. I learned from one of my young men, 15 at the time, who witnessed his father being killed and would later have to testify against the person who killed him. The pressure, the fear, the conflict it built in him while he tried to figure out what to do were huge. I also learned of a young man who was born out of an incestual relationship and was unaware of it for a very long time. His family and the community he resided in knew but did not tell him. When he did find out, it did nothing but eat at him, and to this day, it continues to do so. So many thoughts of how they were failed run through my head. For the young man who witnessed a family member being killed at age 8 – where did the system provide oversight? Then I say, "ok, let me plead ignorance. Suppose no one knew he witnessed a murder, was no adult able to pick up on behaviors?" We do pick up on behaviors, but only the ones we choose to see and then condemn. For many of the young people I work with who have witnessed acts of violence, all have one thing in common. The inability to sleep. Most people who are not getting enough sleep present as tired, irritated, restless, lacking focus, or incoherent. But society says they are rude, ignorant, aggressive, stupid, then give them all of these labels which get trapped in their files and follow them. But, I ask myself, "How many of them really took the time to ask the questions and were patient to wait for the answer?" My other young man whose mother was raped by a relative, who intervened and supported this mother? She didn't ask to be a mother and because of how young she was, did not realize she was pregnant until late in the pregnancy. Did the doctors ask the right questions? Where was law enforcement then? Who taught this young woman what it was to be a mother and to care for another life? All of these stories bring me back to my time in the child welfare system and seeing the long history on each case.

God tells us to honor our mother and father because of the risk we face in not doing so. Our parents may have given birth to us, but it was for God's purpose and glory. We were born for a reason and, as I am learning, in the right season. If God allowed it to happen, it is because He had a purpose and a plan for us. He clearly tells us in Jeremiah 1:5 (NIV), "Before I formed you in the womb, I knew you, / before you were born, I set you apart; / I appointed you as a prophet to the nations."

Again, the greatness of our young people is not being developed because they are not being taught who they are. They believe in the evil that exists, so it is not lost that they would hope in a savior and an all-loving God. Our children are waiting on those who know what love with no condemnation or judgement looks like. But where will they see it? Where will they hear it? And who will show it to them?

It reminds me of Luke 10:25-37 (NIV), the parable of the Good Samaritan:

> On one occasion an expert in the law stood up to test Jesus. "Teacher," he asked, "what must I do to inherit eternal life?"
>
> "What is written in the Law?" he replied. "How do you read it?"
>
> He answered, "'Love the Lord your God with all your heart and with all your soul and with all your strength and with all your mind; and, 'Love your neighbor as yourself.'"
>
> "You have answered correctly," Jesus replied. "Do this and you will live."
>
> But he wanted to justify himself, so he asked Jesus, "And who is my neighbor?"
> In reply Jesus said: "A man was going down from Jerusalem to Jericho, when he was attacked by robbers. They stripped him of his clothes, beat him and went away, leaving him half dead. A priest happened to be

going down the same road, and when he saw the man, he passed by on the other side. So too, a Levite, when he came to the place and saw him, passed by on the other side. But a Samaritan, as he traveled, came where the man was; and when he saw him, he took pity on him. He went to him and bandaged his wounds, pouring on oil and wine. Then he put the man on his own donkey, brought him to an inn and took care of him. The next day he took out two denarii and gave them to the innkeeper. 'Look after him,' he said, 'and when I return, I will reimburse you for any extra expense you may have.'

"Which of these three do you think was a neighbor to the man who fell into the hands of robbers?"

The expert in the law replied, "The one who had mercy on him."

Jesus told him, "Go and do likewise."

If we take a close look at this parable and look at the context that this parable is told, it reads as this to me.

Societal Standards:
Priest/Pastors/Reverends/Bishops—Ordained Levite/Church Congregation and Parishioners—Religious Samaritan (All of us)—Relationship/Spiritual

Although, I would not agree that all priests, pastors, reverends, or faith leaders who have taken an oath would ignore the hurt, bruised, and desolate. I do not think all those who are part of a congregation or church family, which makes up the body of Christ would avoid those same people either, and I certainly do not agree that all who claim to be a child of God would exude the characteristics of the biblical Good Samaritan either. What I am saying is we as a whole, as a society, need to do better. Our young people are waiting on us; they are looking to us not by what we say, but by our fruits.

When the world breaks us, it is meant to condemn us, leave us feeling inadequate and hopeless. It is to destroy our inner being and core. That is not loving; that is not a demonstration of mercy, which God gives us so graciously.

When God breaks us, it is meant to expose the hindrance in our breakthrough. God exposes the sins and uses them to heal us in order for us to walk in the purpose and destiny He created for us. If we are to break, it should be for Him and by Him. His breaking restores us and makes us whole. The world breaks and shatters us and leaves us to pick up the pieces, which we do to our own detriment.

CHAPTER 7

The Light

Purpose … outcome: what is that for me? What is that for this book and for the readers? I wrote this because it was my way of telling the truth as I see it, exposing tactics I believe the enemy is using. Obedience was the other part of the purpose, as it was required of me to demonstrate vulnerability, and humility to share in the experiences and journey He has set for me. Recently, I was praying with fellow believers. As I prayed for direction on my work, understanding on what is currently going on in this country, and where He is, He showed me images of those around Jesus, some kneeling and some standing, some weeping and some staring and this is what came to me: Many speak of the Resurrected Jesus, the glory, the hope and the joy, but many do not speak of the Jesus of the Cross. God is the God of both. He was with Jesus through all of it, through the condemnation, ridicule, slandering, defamation of His character, and every diabolical tactic the enemy threw His way. Jesus, exposed, naked and torn, prayed. He asked His father to forgive them for they know not what they do. It was also my way of shedding His light. Although this is told through a spiritual lens and perspective, and I would love for it to be a foundation for readers. More than anything I ask that you take away a sense of understanding of how these young people have become so dark. Our country is in the midst of these perils, with many under the perception that life is expendable because of what we have shown through racial ignorance, prejudicial systems and laws, but, worst of all, pride and ego. This current generation continues to be lost and is wandering through the wilderness and there are few who have light leading and showing them the way. Society has become tolerant and desensitized to the darkness. We pick and choose who we hold accountable. I do not believe we do well with accountability

Before I dive into accountability, I want to express that we know the difference between right and wrong. We all have our loose definitions of right and wrong, good and bad, kindness and evil—but do we know the difference between being a good person and being a Christian, the child of God we are called to be? Are we ready to be delivered? To be delivered is to eliminate the unclean spirits, the sins we have within our own life. I repeat again, Ephesians 6:12 tells us that, "We wrestle not against flesh and blood, but against principalities, against powers, against the rulers of the darkness of this world" (KJV).

Darkness exists, and God tells us that the physical bodies and what we see are not what our enemy is. It is what we cannot see that brings forth power and darkness. Sometimes we wonder why we make strides in going forward, only at times to fall steps behind. It is the enemy that resides within us that hinders our walk and distorts our views. We are unable to fight darkness if we do not have the light. Jesus is that light.

The world we currently live in is filled with emotional and unstable beings, and our children have suffered as a result of it. "(NKJV) Jesus said to him, I am the way, the truth, and the life. No one comes to the father except through me." My hope, is everyone, especially these young men, will get to know Jesus, His promises, His truth and the way to Eternal life. We live in a world far removed from God. As the world continues to progress with new technology, innovation, scientific medical break-throughs, and change, we adapt and accept. However, His word, the Bible, continues to be challenged. We live in a fallen world, where free will has become distorted with the enemies' manipulation, that salvation seems unimaginable.

For us to be who we were created to be, to make change, to love those around us, to build others up, and, most importantly, to guide the next generation, we need to do our own work and rid ourselves of our Goliaths and our own demons. It is easy to say that you want to walk in courage, and boldness, and that you surrender your life to Him, but control is a stronghold and tactic the enemy uses to convince us that we know best. It is a way of protecting ourselves and that if we do not protect us, no one will. The truth is that we can only trust others to be who they are, and that is human. Because they are human, they will disappoint and let us down, and they will choose themselves before choosing others. Knowing that does not allow for us to relinquish control so easily, which is why it's the biggest stronghold within us. Over the last few months, I had to do some extremely hard work. After God showed me where I was falling short, where some of those sins and unclean spirits were dwelling, I had to make the decision of whether I was going to get delivered in order to produce the fruit my young people need.

I mention accountability, and I hold myself true to that. I have to, in order to hold my young people accountable as well. Although my young people and this generation are in chaos, it does not mean that they are not accountable for change. Once they are being fed in truth, loved without condemnation, and can see another way, we still have a duty to hold them accountable. We do that lovingly and with no judgment. We do that patiently and consistently. At times, we do a disservice to young people when we excuse the things they do because of guilt or sorrow for their situation. We may feel those things, but it does not do anything for them but give them a way out, as well as open the door for manipulation and more of the enemy's spirits to play.

Each generation to come after will be worse than the one before if we do not change trajectories now.

Our world is so full of being noticed, wanting recognition, and needing elevation that people will seek those goals at a cost. This same ideal has taken form in our young people's lives; the articulation of it looks different and they claim it to be respect. They are looking to be noticed, and they are looking for recognition -- positive or negative -- and, of course, validation. They are not being seen for their potential or who they can become in their homes, schools, and community. They are left with having to seek an identity on their own since those around them did not make the time to learn their dreams, the hopes they had, and the wants they have for their lives.

Our young people are looking for anything or anyone who will give them a sense of purpose without understanding what purpose is. Our children do not recognize the value in themselves. They cling to those around them for some form of fulfillment. They feed off the fear they can instill in others, which gives them a false sense of power. But the actions they are take leave them with an empty feeling because it has not replaced the understanding of self, purpose, and destiny. They are searching for answers that can't be found in the street.

God did not call us for religion. God's desire is to have a relationship with us. God wants to spend time with us, get to know us as we are, and for us to lean on Him for any and everything. He tells us, "Come to me, all you who are weary and burdened, and I will give you rest" (Matthew 11:28 NIV). We were not meant to go through life on our own. Our purpose and our story are for someone else. I am reminded of Christ's humility. Criticized and scrutinized every day, He never let that steer Him away from the work that needed to be done. If Christ were to command respect from each and every person, He would not have made it far or completed His purpose.

Why is it that our young people are looking to earn something that we do not deserve? Our young people are craving this recognition, this "respect," yet they do not know what that is. Our young people do not have the capacity to understand that being themselves is enough. Respect is not something that is commanded, but earned through actions, words, and behaviors. Christ never ordered or commanded people to listen or follow Him. What Jesus knew, and we now know, is that "Death and Life are in the power of the tongue, and those who love it will eat its fruit" (Proverbs 18:21 NKJV). Words have the most power over us, yet we cannot seem to grasp that. Our words can cut through another person's soul and do just as much damage as any bullet piercing through flesh. If that were not so, I would not be watching my young people die over what they say. In this current world, social media has become the grand playground for the devil. It gives power, leverage and a platform for all types of "words" to be said and seen. It feeds into his plans of causing everyone to fall. These young people who have grown up never feeling seen or heard, now have the whole world at their fingertips. They use it as their stage to gain power, which is exactly what "he" wants. And then they are killed for it. If words did not matter, if it did not damage, if it did not have power, why would it cause someone to be engulfed in enough rage to kill someone? Why would it build hate within anyone to have that person spend the time and energy to seek that individual who is just spewing "words?" They have not physically touched them, they did not stand face to face with them, but what it did was embed "his spirit" within that person. All he needs is a window or a door to be let in. Once he is in, he is able to wreak havoc, and build upon his playground. Hear me when I say this, if God speaks of His fruits, you must know the devil has his as well. The devil wants what God has, which is His power and His children. So, everything God has created, each of His words He has left us in His word, the devil has his as well.

We lack the ability and the power to save or help ourselves. When we learn that we cannot overcome this world on our own, our life begins to change. When our young people begin to put their trust and faith in God, when they learn how to suit themselves in the armor of the Lord, they will win the battle. Understanding that every day is a battle, our young people can begin to walk in the confidence and assurance of the Lord. That walk will begin to lead them into their destiny and into their purpose. Not every day or every battle will require them to suit up in God's armor, but after they grow strong in their minds and are filled with His truth, they will begin to discern which battles are for them and which battles are for God to fight. I pray that this happens sooner rather than later. One of the questions I have for God is this; if my young people die before they know You, will they end up with You? A young man I met three years ago on the pretrial unit who was being convicted of murder, and was found guilty was recently killed. I have lost young people before, but his death hit me differently. Although he was guilty of his actions, it was seen as an accident. To protect him and his family, I will not go into much detail. What I can share was the pain each day this young man lived with because of his actions. That year I spent getting to know him, I am not sure how much he actually slept because he shared with me each time he would go to sleep he would relive the scene and the pain. When I heard of his death, I couldn't believe it. Partly because I heard about it a few months after it had happened, but also because I was not made aware that he was released. His death was captured on social media, and that brought upon even more pain.

I am 35 and still learning which battles are mine and which ones belong to the Lord. Most of our battles are His, but there are some He will allow us to fight on our own when He feels we have the knowledge to do so. Everyone's battles are going to look different, and our young people will have to learn that. Their environment may look similar to others', their stories might sound familiar to their friends', but believe me when I say our battles are going to be different, and we have to have faith in God to give us the strength to fight them. He tells us that He does not give us more than we can handle.

What others say about our character has the power to cut us deep because we start to believe it. We hurt more when those closest to us begin to devalue us and strip our dignity from us. Understanding one's purpose can take years. I even believe once you do figure it out, you then question it for a bit because you start to ask, "Are you sure, Father?" I have done that many times, and each time, I swear He is shaking His head at me. He has made it loud and clear, "Janelle, you are here for souls." Let me be clear: I am not making any reference or statement to being Jesus, but we are called to be a fisher of men. God has blessed me with an ability to connect with young people, to build relationships and trust, and, most importantly, to encourage them to do differently and to be a blessing in various ways to them. I am able to sit and talk with them in a way that allows for trust to be instilled in the moment. The space is safe enough that they can ask questions and listen to another perspective. I have been genuine with each young person I meet with the statement that before any role I play, I am a mother first. I love and treat you no differently than how I treat my own child. The same decisions I want and make for you would be the ones I make for the person I gave birth to. The challenges I have faced along the way for being a woman and working with young impressionable males has not been easy, but because I know my intent and God knows my heart, I continue to push through.

When I look into the face of my young ones, I see confusion. I believe they do not know how they ended up in this situation, but they have learned to adapt to circumstances being what they are. For me to tell them that the devil has waged war and he is using them as his soldiers would leave them feeling like a thing instead of a person. Besides the fact that they question whether God exists, it leaves me pained because if they do not believe in God, then they can't see that a devil exists. If they can't see that he exists, they can't fight him. It means they leave themselves exposed and wide open, which is dangerous but a joy for the enemy.

Please, take a look at what our country is going through. Our young black and brown men are dying. Our black and brown men have a bounty on their heads with no explanation of how they have gotten there. Nothing happening in our world should be a surprise. Even if you are not an historian, even if you do not believe in the living God, at least take a moment to look around. Question what you see and what you hear, and then ask yourself, who would want to wake up one day and live a life of misery, hate, and anger? Who would want to live a life where theirs and others' lives can be disregarded and disposable? That seems so evil.

Our young people, who do not have all of the information and no knowledge of the real battle, have decided that they are capable of making life decisions. They get to decide how to handle someone who has wronged them. That decision can become life or death. Some of our young people have decided they can play God. They do not see that they have been held in bondage and captivity to the thoughts the devil has placed inside their heads, telling them, "It is not fair," and having them question every situation that crosses them. He makes them believe if they do not make a wrong right, or if they do not get even with someone, it will diminish them. Our young boys have decided that if they do not kill the other person, they will be killed. They have targeted each other, rather than who the real enemy is. Our young people think they may be winning a war on the streets, but do they really know they are losing the battle of their minds? Do they fully understand that they are not the ones in control?

What I see as the challenge with accepting Christ is this, if you ask people, do they want to go to Heaven, they say yes. Even if they question whether God exists, and aren't entirely sure there is a Heaven, they want to go. If you ask them about salvation, there lies the push-back and scrutiny. For young people who insist they have the answer to everything at the tip of their finger, salvation can translate to power. Putting hope into a "being" they cannot see is unthinkable for them especially when they put hope into people they can see. People often mistake what "faith" and "salvation" are.

Christ has told us that our Heavenly Father, who is King of all high, has created us in His image to be a blessing. We are the princes and princesses of the Highest, and until we know that, we will never settle into our destiny or purpose.

When we can stand firm in who we are, we can walk intelligently in our ways. It won't matter what anyone says about us because we will not waver like the sea or be of double mind to question our worth. It is then our young men can stand boldly and walk in confidence that their future is promising, as long as they continue to have hope and faith.

People often confuse what it is to be a Christian or the role a Christian is to play. The mistake is that we think we have to earn our way into heaven. It wasn't until I was in church and my pastor's sermon lit a light in my head and painted the picture clear enough for me see. We have two belief systems, he stated, belief on "what do I have to do to please God?" and "celebrate what God has done for me." Those who follow religion believe in the first statement, which means they have to come to God with it all figured out and perfected. Those who have a relationship with Christ, and understand what it means to be a Christian, understand the second statement, which means being thankful for what Christ has done and continues to do for us. God was intentional about how He was going to save His children. John 3:16 -- the most well-known verse Scripture -- states, "God so loved the world, that he gave his one and only Son, that whoever believes in him shall not perish but have eternal life" (NIV).

We continue to prove by the way our society is shaped that we do not understand God and Jesus. More than 2,000 years later, His love is still unclear, so let me help make it a bit clearer for you. God came in human form, as Jesus Christ, and showed us what love, relationship, and compassion were. Our world then, and now, was filled with so much evil, chaos, and confusion over who God was that He saw no other way. As a loving parent, He decided to save His children by being intentional in all that He did and intentional in all that He continues to do. It is significant to remember, however, that the enemy is also intentional. The strategies he uses are to implore the world in its righteousness and continue to whisper in the ears of those who are seeking power and fulfillment. God's words tell us of His love for His children. His mercy He gives us each day shows us that His love is everlasting. Both in the Old Testament and the New Testament, He expresses His Love. In Deuteronomy (Old Testament) 7:9,

"Know therefore that the Lord your God is God; he is the faithful God, keeping his covenant of love to a thousand generations of those who love him and keep his commandment" (NIV)

and in Romans (New Testament) 8:37-39,

"No, in all these things we are more than conquerors through him who loves us. For I am convinced that neither death nor life, neither angels nor demons, neither the present nor the future, nor any powers, neither height nor depth, nor anything else in all creation, will be able to separate us from the love of God that is in Christ Jesus our Lord." (NIV)

Our purpose and our story are for someone else with His guidance. People make the statements that "religious people are hypocrites" and that people act one way in church and another in their personal lives. Although that might be true for many people, the ones making those statements have already demonstrated that they do not know God or His wants for us. It is not for us to judge the actions of others. It is not for us to condemn those who choose to live certain ways; it is for us to love them and point them in His direction when they begin to wander too far off their given path.

Our children are dying; My work for the past 14 years has shown me this. Our children are not making it, and this is our fault. We are not being intentional anymore in how we reach our young ones. We have allowed society to decide how our children should be raised, taught, walk, talk, act, and decide who they are. When did it become all right for society to decide who our children are? Better yet, when did we allow society to decide who they are not? Black and brown children are only seeing the worst images of themselves, being educated by those who do not believe in them, and, on top of it all, have to face their inner demon in their minds convincing them that they are not worth it. It is no wonder they are not making it!

We have had more black and brown people incarcerated than the number of slaves during the 1800s. How is that possible? Where is our progress? The physical cuffs came off, but the bond and captivity were never released. People of color have not come together strong enough to fight the battles the enemy has created. The faction and division among people of color is deplorable and causes our young people to see the disingenuous love we have for one another. The dissension among us is visible to the world and continues to be our stumbling block. We have allowed society to convince us that we need to adhere to certain standards in order to rise in position and power. The enemy continues to stay true to his name as the accuser and has allowed us to continue passing judgment on those who look like us and those who don't.

Unfortunately, we have become more critical of our own kind, which binds the progress we could be making in this country. Until we are able to put the greater good before our own selfishness, we will not break the systemic oppression and the barriers that continue to plague black and brown folks in this country. The enemy knows that if he continues to fill us with the poisons of the spirit, like envy, jealousy, hatred, discord, lust, and idolatry (see Galatians 5), we will never be able to fight united and with power. If the enemy continues to keep black and brown people filled with bitterness and rage because of our continued plight, we will question an all-loving God. We will not seek His face for answers or rest, but we will rest in our own power and beliefs. Again, the enemy knows the lies he needs to create, the boundaries to separate us, and the embedding of opposition among us. If we are to change the paths of young people, we have to walk by action and create the unity we wish to see. Because we have not done that, we continue to perpetuate the violence, the trauma, the oppression, and the generational dysfunction, which leaves our young people confused, lost, and hopeless.

This generation has come into a time where a sense of entitlement is driving the decisions they make. Our children are being led to believe that they are owed something. Whether it is respect, loyalty, or fear, they insist it is owed to them. I would like to know who lied to our young people and told them this. Nothing is owed to them, but yes, we have failed them. We have not taken accountability for our actions and the part we play in society. The fear and the insecurities the enemy has planted in us have landed our young people where they are. The inability to trust one another, to love one another, and to lift each other, especially as people of color, has been our greatest downfall and, therefore, a broken commandment that the Lord has given us.

Despite all of this, my hope still lies within Him. Our Father says, in 2 Chronicles 7:14, "If my people, who are called by name will humble themselves, and pray, and seek my face, and turn from their wicked ways; then will I hear from heaven, and will forgive their sin, and will heal their land" (2 Chronicles 7:14 NKJV)

On the end of the millennial spectrum, I know in my generation there are many of us who were raised in the church, but there were many who were not. In the 80's when the war on drugs epidemic hit this nation, many were raised filled with the spirts of the streets. Watching drugs, and watching our black and brown people dying or being taken off to jail was the onset of these spirts. I was 4years old when I saw just how methodical these unclean spirts were. As I was home with my grandmother, and looked outside the window, I remember watching a tall black man with a high-top haircut, puke green trench coat walk gracefully down my street. I see another black man get off the porch next door to my house, start walking towards this man, yelling and screaming at him. I remember the man with the trench coat pull a long gun out of the inside of his jacket and began to shoot the other man and his body go down. I do not remember what happened after that, but I remember my grandmother grabbing me from the window, so I did not see what happened next. More than 30 years later, those images are still burned in my head, at times a bit fuzzy, but I still remember what the gunman looked like. Being older now, I know that the gun was a rifle, and the men were young men, and if I had to guess age, late adolescence. My mother came home to yellow tape around our house, and cops. She asked my grandmother what happened, and recalls me saying "boom-boom" and gesturing with my hands as a gun. That is all it took for my mother to move my brother and me out of that neighborhood in Boston. I mention this about myself because these are the images young people see more than once, and more than twice with the inability to change their surroundings. I had mentioned that the murder of one of my young men was captured on social media. I was sent the video clip of it, and had debated for several days on whether I should watch it. Just like the murder of George Floyd and countless others, it is the reality of our young people who are exposed to these images repeatedly. They do not always get a choice in what they witness. Some place themselves in those parameters, while others just happen to be in the wrong place at the wrong time. Removing any image of darkness from your head is difficult, and the longer it is able to stay there, the more distorted he can make it. The video was two minutes, but took me four days to make it to the end of the clip. What I choose to remember is seeing his face with his friends, acting silly, talking nonsense and garbage as most young men do. But what I also remember is hearing the panic in his friend's voices when they realized he was shot, and that he was unresponsive, asking him to wake up.

If no one is reaching these young men, and giving light to that darkness, how is His truth able to clear the way?

The one blessing I am beyond grateful for is my son. I gave my son to the Lord when he was born, and have not steered from that. No matter how tired I was, or am, church was a must on Sundays. Reading Bible stories to him from the time he was born was something that not only I did, but both of his grandmothers as well. Proverbs 22:6 says "train up a child in the way he should go and when he gets older he will not depart from it." (NKJV) I am not naïve to believe that when my son hits his phases in life, that it is possible that he will wander off his path. But because that foundation has been laid, I know he will return to it. I had wandered off, and have ventured back because I know this world, and His plan is bigger than me. If there is one thing I will know leaving this earth, is that I gave my son the best thing I could give him, which is Jesus Christ. I did not give him religion, because there is more to the foundation than having him attend church and read his Bible, but spending time speaking to the lord and knowing that my son is watching my relationship with Christ as well. What he chooses to do as he gets older will be on him as he begins his walk.

My prayer is that my generation and the ones that come after will soon venture back soon to this path. My fear is that there will be an emptiness within the church because there was no foundation laid. The current generation and their families are not in the churches. I should be clear on when I say church, that I am not necessarily referring to a building or a place, but rather the body of people in Christ. Many would argue that you do not need to be in a physical location to worship and spend time with Christ, and I would whole heartedly agree. However, there is an overwhelming feeling you receive when you are in a place for Him. My church is a sanctuary for me. When I step into the pew (same seat for the past 5 years) there is a calming spirit and a sense of relief that sweeps over me. I feel like I am home, and no one else during that time exists. It's also accountability for me. When I am watching service online, there isn't anyone there to ask me, "how are you doing?". Anywhere else, I can say, I am ok, or I am good. In church, I can't say that, especially if my pastor asks me. Is it that I am lying when others ask me? I don't believe I am. It's that I feel safer saying it to the pastors in church. If I am not ok, it will lead me to evaluating what is going on with me, and the changes I need to make. Again, accountability. If I am not ok, I risk making decisions that are harmful for those around me.

We will have to give an account of every word we speak on our day of judgement. Matthew 12: 36-37 tells us, "But I say to you that for every idle word men may speak, they will give an account of it in the day of judgement." For by your words you will be justified, and by your words you will be condemned (NKJV) There are two things I believe God is going to ask us when we are before Him: 1) What did you do with the time I gave you? 2) Who knew you because of me? Paul gives us an example of how to best use our time. He says in 1 Corinthians 9:19-23 (NKJV) "For though I am free from all men, I have myself a servant to all, that I might win the more, and to the Jews I became like a Jew, that I might win the Jews; to those who are under the law, as under the law, to those who are without law, as without law (not being without law toward God but under law toward Christ), that I might win those who are under without law; to the weak I became as weak, that I might win the weak. I have become all things to all men, that I might by all means save some. Now this I do for the gospels sake, that I may be partaker of it with you. "

Being a woman has always had its blessings and curses. Some may argue that it is because Eve had tasted the "forbidden fruit" and cursed the lineage of women to come. Others would argue that it was her weakness for falling prey to the enemy that therefore brought upon destruction not only on herself but on man as well. This battle over the power of women has always been an ongoing debate that I believe will never be resolved. Pauls' message was for everyone, not just men, but women and children as well. At least, not until we get to ask her ourselves, "What really happened in that garden?"

What I do know is that the power of women continues to be an ongoing debate between both sexes, including those who identify in other ways or other categories. I am here to discuss with you the power of women who are called to shepherd while being a sheep and following after Christ. Being a sheep in a world that does not know our Heavenly Father is incredibly hard, but on top of that, to be a shepherd adds another layer. Now, being a shepherd in heels (which would be me), well, it makes it almost impossible. You are constantly going against the norm (societal norm, not God's norm), and everyone has different views of what the norm is. From the world, there is one set; from the church, another; religion, there is another norm (notice how I separate church and religion); and in your own family is another. One of the bigger challenges is that we have our own definition of what the "norm" looks like because we pick and choose from every area to create our own. The Bible warns of conforming, and that this world is temporary.

When God gives you your mission and deploys you, every barrier, obstacle, and enemy comes your way. When you have a heart for the work, He gives you the strength and a "machete" to chop your way through all of the chaos and noise. Even in the moments you become weary and feel like giving up, you find a renewed sense of strength, so you put your heels on again, you armor yourself with His truth, and you head out. When you stay in the fight for more than a decade, and the world's voice begins to grow stronger and stronger, hearing His becomes harder, and it's more faint because of the loudness of other "worldly competition." It's a struggle to drown out everything else and focus on His words. When His voice becomes difficult to hear, using yours gets lost. The voice He gave you becomes so faded that you question whether you are using it at all, and the choices and decisions you make start to spiral and align more with the world's than His.

So, I am speaking to all my fellow shepherds out there. Whether you are in heels or not, I encourage you to hold on because His presence is here. His voice is here. He has not gone anywhere, and His voice has not changed. In a world with noise cancellation headsets, we need to put on a pair of Beats and tune in to Him. He has reminded me there are more of me out there, and the remainder of His work needs to be made known. So, here I am, introducing myself as a Shepherd in Heels, sharing my walk with Him, my faith in Him, the fight I see in this world, and the enemy's war for our black and brown children's souls. My hope is that this resonates with others and encourages others that they are not alone in some of these battles. We are distracted at times by what society says and does rather than looking to the cross, remembering His word and embedding Him in our hearts. Understanding that before we can heal our children, we need to begin to recognize and see the pain, the persecution we have allowed in this world. We have to get down on our knees and be vulnerable, ask to be searched to expose those dark areas the enemy resides in. Then, we need to be humble ourselves and ask for forgiveness, and reclaim our battlefield.

So, I ask you this: If He is for us, who can be against us? I am here for souls, are you?

CPSIA information can be obtained
at www.ICGtesting.com
Printed in the USA
LVHW030522221220
674783LV00003B/432